Windward
Family

Windward Family

An atlas of love, loss
and belonging

ALEXIS KEIR

THREAD

This edition published by Thread in 2023

An imprint of Storyfire Ltd.
Carmelite House
50 Victoria Embankment
London EC4Y 0DZ

www.thread-books.com

ISBN: 978-1-90977-071-3
eBook ISBN: 978-1-80019-959-0

The names of some individuals have been
changed in order to protect their privacy.

The review of *Fatherland* in 'Dance, Dance, Dance' was previously
published by *The London Magazine* in 2018. They retain copyright and the
review been reproduced with their permission.

'Talk Radio' was previously published as 'I Lands' by *The Selkie* in 2019.

'Keep The Faith' was previously recorded in audio as 'From A Distance' for
We've Chosen Here in 2020.

'My Girlfriend Cuts My Hair' was previously published in the 35th
edition of *The Caribbean Writer* in 2021.

Printed and bound in Great Britain

The FSC® label means that materials used for the product
have been responsibly sourced.

MIX
Paper from
responsible sources
FSC® C104740

To Lin and Win

Tell a story.
Bobby Womack

Sometimes we lose one of our own because we do not tell them enough that no matter how far they have been flung to the ends of the universe we still love them.
Witi Ihimaera – The Dream Swimmer

Nga taonga o nga tupuna tuku iho kia koe – The treasures of your ancestors must be passed on to you.
Shared by Murray Ryburn

Contents

Note: Regarding references to New Zealand/Aotearoa, I have followed the University of Canterbury convention: 'Aotearoa New Zealand' on first use and thereafter 'Aotearoa'.

PREFACE

Lin

1962, Islington

She is so excited. She stares at her reflection in the mirror propped in front of her and feels so proud of the badge pinned to her breast pocket which reads 'Pupil Midwife' in tight black type. As proud as if it were a medal. One worth far more than those she used to win for her school back home. Everyone she has written to since she passed through Preliminary Training School has received a black-and-white photograph of her in her student nurse uniform – not smiling but her expression and eyes lit by her new stature, half turned to the invisible cameraman as she sits on a stool in a draughty Archway hall.

The crisp, white linen of her dress accentuates the shadows which cast the rest of the room into grey and black. Her notebook is open on the small wooden desk which is the room's only furniture aside from the neatly made bed, which she will soon tumble into even as the noises outside increase on this grey, North London morning. The pillow on it is the one she brought all the way from the Caribbean. Out of custom, all the Vincentians who travelled overseas always carried their own, and she has not been separated from it since she stood on the dock at Kingstown waiting to squeeze onto the Geest ship, which would carry a cargo of migrants and bananas eastwards and onwards to Tilbury.

Each pair of lined pages in the notebook is headlined by the title 'Delivery No.' and she is completing her record of the night's arrivals and observations. Names, ages, number of pregnancies regardless of outcome – the lives of four women mapped through maternity. Five new lives brought into the world, one arriving only after trauma. Duration of labour, sex, weight, length and head circumference all carefully noted. And condition: 'good, cried at once', 'both satisfactory', 'mother satisfactory'… 'baby resuscitated with O_2 successfully'.

On the bed is a still unfinished aerogramme – she will complete it when she wakes in the afternoon. She was writing home again. Telling Mummy and her sisters about this cold, cold country. About how she loved her studies and how different it felt to again be a student sitting behind a desk. And that she was working hard to justify the money they had all saved to send her here. She knew they would be interested to know how hard it had been to find Caribbean food until she found out that if she caught two buses, she could get to a place called Hackney and go to Chatsworth Road or Ridley Road markets. She would tell them about the other student nurses, including the West Indians who she spent a lot of time with, a Grenadian girl and one from Saint Lucia. The 'Windward Ladies' was what they called themselves, giggling as they chatted in the cafeteria.

One Saturday night they had taken her to a late-night dance down some stairs from the pavement near Alexandra Palace, the *first club she had ever been to. She stood by the wall shyly while the other two older girls, who were nearly thirty, flirted and danced. She would not tell Mummy too much about that.*

But a tall, skinny boy with a full head of Brylcreemed hair had asked where she was from, and when she replied he had said, 'Wha'! I is a Vincy too!' She knew her sisters' eyes would open wider at that, and they would be gripped by the fact that the boy was from Biabou, not too far down the coast from Georgetown. She already knew a little about his family simply because he had so many brothers and cousins.

He was a country boy, but he told her that he wanted to become an architect, although right now he was working on the railways. 'Just for now till t'ings come tru, yuh understan'?' He was a little forward and bold with himself, and after she held his hand on the dance floor, she could smell the oil of the locomotives on her fingers. But he was good-looking, and it felt nice for someone to make her laugh out loud again.

Before taking off her uniform and slipping under the sheet and blanket of the narrow bed, she marked a date in black ballpoint in her small turquoise nurses diary. It would be two more weeks before she would be free on a Saturday night and could go back to the club, but if he was there, she knew she would let him dance with her again.

Barrels

Heathrow Airport in 1974 was where the first unzipping of our family began. That was the year my sister and brother – Alison and Anthony – and I were sent to the island of Saint Vincent to stay with a relative of our father whilst my mother travelled to Fort Worth, Texas to work as a nurse. Our dad stayed behind in Luton to sell our house. The plan and aspiration were for us all to move to the States in search of a better life. My brother, sister and I were in Saint Vincent for about a year, and after that it took two decades for me to travel back to find the parts of myself I had left behind in the Caribbean.

At the airport I screamed. Tears, wails and snot wrenched and tunnelled their way out of a well deep within me, deeper than it seemed a small boy's frame could possibly sustain and definitely more than it could contain. My brother and sister, too young to understand what was happening, cried too, following my example. But their tears did not split the air in the departure lounge nor penetrate the disinterested chatter in the air-conditioned hum around us.

I did not just wail. It was my screams which shook other travellers out of the peace and sanctity of their own reunions and farewells. They looked at me and then looked away again because they knew they had no permission or power to do anything. As awful as it was, this disturbance – this tearing apart of parents and children – was sanctioned. All they saw was a small boy in distress as the lady from the cabin crew led me gently by the hand through the gates, and the figures of my mother and father receded behind us.

I do not remember anything of the flight: what food we ate or which films the cabin crew tried to use to distract three children aged ten, six and three in their grief. Did we sleep fitfully or simply cry and cling on to each other for all of the six-hour flight to Barbados? Who helped us and our luggage through transit when we got there? All these things were ill remembered, and in the grey fuzz of my memories, the figures who met us at the end were just grown-up, indistinct shadows.

I grew up thinking that only my sister and brother could carry with me the burdens of being separated from our parents as children. But one quiet Friday in 2017 in Hornsey, as I worked on my laptop and listened to the radio, I heard the childhood memories of other adults who had been left behind with relatives whilst their mothers and fathers travelled overseas to set up base camp for a better life. 'Barrel children' – I had not even known that there was a label for what had happened to us.

Hearing stories that mirrored ours brought connection and comfort, just like the clothes and gifts we had eagerly waited for from our parents, packed and sent over in time for Christmas and birthdays in the same big tubs that held the food and goods sent back regularly to the people caring for us. Journeys travelled and forgotten came back to me beckoned by the voices on the radio. I heard the stories of other adults who felt that they had been set adrift as children, and finally, decades later and battered by uncertainty, I understood my own experience of separation and loss. There was a thick, black journal in a drawer in my flat, stuffed with letters, postcards, handwritten notes and diary entries. For the first time in years, I opened it.

Catherine

July 1808, Saint Vincent

The sea roared off the windward coast, and the noise seemed louder in the darkness of night when only the white froth of the waves was visible. Ramshackle huts lined the coast, half hidden in the bush. They clustered around the bends where rock-lined streams had finished their journey down from the mountain and crept out into the Atlantic. On the beaches, broken fronds of coconut palm lined the boundary between black sand and sea.

On bright days, the sky could be so clear at Colonarie that the slaves loading sugar cane onto ships bound for Kingstown might see the shape of Saint Lucia in the distance, its hills and contours faint through the sea mist. But six o'clock had passed and night had fallen quickly, the sky black and heavy with cloud. On the plantation, faint points of candlelight escaped through the planks of all the huts, but only one was full of sound and movement.

The enslaved Africans always gathered like this when tragedy struck — although it needed a high mark of suffering to use such a word after they had already endured and somehow survived transportation across the Middle Passage in the dank bowels of the slave ships. A generation before, many had escaped to mingle and resist with the Caribs who, refusing to accept subjugation, defiantly and bloodily resisted the British from the mountain valleys and forests of their invaded island before eventual defeat and, for many, exile. The Africans called the Carib country 'the land of milk and honey'. Those who remained in slavery still found ways to cling together to shoulder the pain that was poured onto their lives.

The women came together when someone was gravely ill or approaching death, like the little girl whose swollen body was carried into her mother's hut after she stumbled into a nest of Jack Spaniard hornets and was stung on every inch of her skin. The girl screamed with every jolt when her bearers stumbled and each shift as her swollen body rolled on the boards they used to carry her back to the village. Those screams becoming strangled and drawn-out moans as her throat closed and her life ebbed away with the women praying around her. Those were the same boards that were used again whenever the sea flung back the still and bloated corpse of a too-adventurous child up or down the coast.

Now the women had come together again, to comfort and hold their own as they had to when they were separated from the men of their villages by fortified barricados below the decks of the slave ships. Wearing robes as long and as clean as they could find, they sang songs carried in their memories from across the ocean, and they swayed together, tear-stained faces illuminated by candles placed on the ground or on the old boxes that served as table and furniture.

There was a knock on the thin door, and the voices quietened as two men came into the crowded hut. The slighter man was called Hardwick, and he was the reverend of this parish of Charlotte, his religion and guidance giving the white colonisers the laws and natural order they demanded from God. He offered 'Good evening, good evening' all around whilst the older and burlier man, the overseer of the plantation, spoke not at all but took guard and stayed behind the light thrown by his oil lantern. The Carib Wars and the fierce resistance of Chatoyer's warriors against the efforts of the British to expand their grip on the island were still fresh in the memory of the estate owners, and the overseer never lowered his guard whenever he was outnumbered by the Africans. His curt nod towards the door he had just come through was enough to tell most of the women to withdraw silently, and then the two figures they had been huddled around became visible. Neither man removed his hat.

A young woman lay on the sweat-stained cloths and sheets that were boxed into a corner of the hut by the remains of a broken-up pallet. She was no older than seventeen years and had been born into slavery on the island. Next to her lay a baby whose body was wrapped in cloths, snuffled against her breast. Only its head was visible, and the reverend could not take his eyes from the baby's black and naked crown, which was mottled with large patches of white. The girl's mother, back bent from her years of labour, leant over her daughter, mopping her brow with water from a cracked enamel bowl.

The overseer's gaze took this all in, and he made a mental note to return the bowl to the plantation house. He thought that these niggers should make do with a calabash like all the rest no matter what lies they told about the parentage of this child.

'Ladies, you know the reason Mr Gratton and I are here...' began the reverend. Although they were alone now, still he spoke in a low whisper.

But the girl's voice cut him off. 'Mammy, mi nah hafi give 'im up.'

'Catherine, shush chile, look 'pon de pickney… 'im mus' hafi be sick, have some disease nah.'

'But is mi chile, Mammy, mi flesh an' blood.'

'Ladies, if I may…' the reverend tried to carry on, but the girl continued her wails over the sound of his voice until the overseer stepped forward and the slight shift in the weight of the presences in the room brought her to a coughing, choking pause. She thought about all the times she and the other slaves had worked in the cane fields with him striding between them, spitting, swearing and lashing out with his club-headed stick for seemingly no reason at all.

'If I may… the Church can ensure a good upbringing for this poor, afflicted infant. And scientific study may well avail society of a cure for the curse of his impediment. A gentleman newly arrived in Kingstown is most interested in what he has heard of the child and is willing to take him back to England for the purposes of research and remediation. That is where the study of such a… a… natural phenomenon… should properly take place for the enlightenment of all mankind.'

The girl cried out again, and her mother fixed the reverend with a stare which caused him to pause and fiddle nervously with his dog collar.

'You have to consider the prospects for him here on the island, fatherless.'

In the shadows there was a grunt and a nod.

'In England he will be safe from ridicule and harm. Why on earth should anyone care about the colour of his skin there? Mr Alexander

worries about how the other estate labourers will react. They are backward and superstitious…' The reverend seemed to forget that the only human support available to the two women had been forced to leave them the moment he and the overseer had come in.

'Mi nah hafi consider anything! He ah mi chile!'

'Shush, baby, shush, nah work yourself up so. The reverend ah simply try fi find a way forward.'

'Mummy, mi cyannnnt…'

'As discussed with your mother, your assistance and co-operation will be noted and recognised. It is of course within the rights of the estate to make plans for the child as Mr Alexander wishes, it having been born into his possession. But with compassion and understanding, he has agreed that if you give the child up, then you and your mother shall be granted your liberty.' And he dipped his head in a bow as if to acknowledge thanks which were never offered.

The girl sat up, her movement causing the baby to cry as it was separated from her breast, but then she collapsed back into her mother's arms, which latched around and rocked her.

There was another pause and then the reverend coughed impatiently. 'Shall I take the infant now?'

The old woman's immobility as he reached towards the bed was enough sign for him to assume her agreement. His fingers stretched around the tiny bundle, while the baby's grandmother tightened her grip around her daughter. But still the girl would not let go, and that was the provocation the overseer needed to step into the light, thin strands of red hair falling across his pockmarked face from under his hat.

The girl stared up at him with more than a fieldhand's passing recognition, eyes wide with fright.

'This bastard shall not stay here and blight my good name. Let him go!' he roared, the Scottish tones in his voice harsh and angry.

He pulled the bundle away from her arms with the same shredding force that the slaves used to strip leaves from cane in the fields. Without a backwards look, he stepped away out of the room carrying the baby. The girl's mother released a long, shallow breath of resignation. It was done.

'Yuh ah bring de papers later, Reverend Hardwick? Tomorrow?'

'Yes, and I assure you I will do everything in my power to make the voyage comfortable for the child. The ship will leave from Kingstown next week. A wet nurse has been arranged. And I will ensure regular missives from England about his progress...' If this mistake of God survives at all, he mused internally and silently, without allowing his expression to change.

'Oh Lawd Mudder Gawd. Oh, Gawd have mercy 'pon mi, forgive mi Fadder, forgive mi, forgive mi...'

'Please, please, calm yourself. There is nothing more to be said now. This is a matter for the Lord, His will be done. One final issue though – has the infant been named?'

A whisper came from the girl. 'George. If 'im ah gwan to England call 'im George. After de king so people ah go keep 'im safe and look after 'im.'

A smirk at her simplicity nearly surfaced on the reverend's face, but he managed to suppress it. 'George is a fine name. So be it. George *after the king and Alexander his surname after your benefactor, who has given you honest labour and this shelter to live in.'*

'No.' The grandmother spoke decisively and with finality, her tone brooking no argument. This woman could still faintly remember freedom, and she spoke with the strength and dignity that had been given her by her forebears. 'Gratton. People dem say that de chile nah have no daddy to claim 'im but give 'im de name of de man who ah mek him come so into this worl' and who ah tek him 'way. 'Im name ah go be Gratton.'

Part I

ENGLAND

Annie

In 2015 I was living in Stratford, and my son Tom would come to stay with me every couple of weeks in my small, one-bedroomed flat. Our bicycles were our means of escape from its restricted space, and with them East London was ripe for exploration.

The canals helped us on our adventures: the Lea Navigation running either beyond the North Circular into Hertfordshire and Essex or south down to the Thames and Limehouse Basin, and from there the Regent's Canal offered an alternative route back to Angel. Sometimes we would ride along the Greenway, laid over the four-mile path of the Victorian Northern Outfall Sewer, boring like a giant worm through East London parks and streets from Hackney to Beckton. I had cycled over its traffic- and hill-free gravel dozens of times, using it as a quick way to get to the eastern parts of Newham or to take either of my sons to explore the eerily abandoned and derelict slopes of the Beckton Alps. From the heights up there, East London spread out beneath and around us. The swathes of houses, streets, warehouses and industrial sites were scattered with green, the river threading to the south and the Olympic Stadium and DNA-like strands of the ArcelorMittal Orbit standing like upstart interruptions in Stratford, back the way we had come from.

That May brought the wettest imaginable weekend, but on Sunday there was a pause in the downpours so Tom and I tracked out on our bikes cutting north and east from Stratford along roads through to Cann Hall. That day was when we came across for the first time the ornate gothic splendour of the chapel entrance to West Ham cemetery, which was opened in 1857.

I had always been fascinated by the ring of seven Victorian graveyards which had been created in the nineteenth century in the suburbs which encircled Central London. Not just Highgate Cemetery, the famous resting place of Karl Marx next to Waterlow Park, but also those I had lived or worked near in Tower Hamlets, Stoke Newington and Nunhead. In these graveyards, nature's vines, birds and creeping mammals had invaded to keep company the sinking headstones, weathered tombs and grand mausoleums and to comfort the weeping angels.

We got off our cycles and wheeled them as we walked through the lanes of the cemetery, exclaiming at the age of the dates on the weathered and cracked stone memorials or at how brief some lives had been. We spent some time there on our day of exploration and then we ventured out into the wide-open spaces of Wanstead Flats. On those muddy fields, our bikes were our steeds, and we galloped and cantered, playing chase and sinking our wheels into the water and ooze. We got wet with abandon, simply not caring that our clothes and shoes were soon soaked. At times, the standing water between the trees on the edge of the flats became ponds rather than puddles, and coots floated ahead on the same paths as us as our bikes tried to make headway.

For a little while I left behind everything outside our bike ride. I forgot living alone, forgot the pain of separation and missing my boys. I did not remember that every other weekend I felt utterly lost and without a role to fix my place in the world. Right now, I was happy. It was only when we were nearly across the flats, soaked and grinning foolishly, that a chill sank over me that did not come from being wet. As I watched Tom's dripping and grubby socks and shoes pedalling ahead, a familiar unease returned to whisper to me that perhaps again I had done something wrong. The ornate arch of the entrance to the much larger City of London cemetery was visible ahead, but I called out to Tom, and we turned and headed back.

It was several years later that I found out that within the 200 acres and over 150,000 gravesites of that other vast cemetery was the resting place of someone whose life had traced a path which my own parents later followed.

In 2019, Stephen Bourne, a renowned researcher into the history of Black communities in Britain, travelled to the City of London cemetery in search of the grave of a woman who had been buried there 117 years before. He was looking for the resting place of Annie Brewster, one of the earliest Black people to be recorded as working as a nurse in England. Annie had been buried in the cemetery on 14 February 1902.

The cemetery's administrators expressed strong doubts to Bourne that after such a long period, any physical indication of the grave would remain, but he persisted in his search, guided only by a small site map. After he left the archivists' office where he had been given the map, there was no one around for him to ask for help. But the Victorian burial register had been precise in its record, and Bourne had at least some idea of which areas to try. After searching for several hours, he found what he was looking for.

On that hot August day, Bourne came across a large, heavy stone cross, fallen and deeply buried in thick grass. He had to pull away clumps of the undergrowth to view its full length, and he could see that about a third of the way up it was snapped in two. He needed to use tissues and his spit to make the dedication on the memorial stone at its base visible, but it was there:

ANNIE CATHERINE BREWSTER
(NURSE OPHTHALMIC)
AGED 43 YEARS
WHO DIED 11TH FEBRUARY 1902

Bourne has said that at that moment he felt overwhelming relief and joy, to the point that he was on the verge of tears. When I heard about Annie's story from newspaper articles and from Stephen, I too experienced immense feelings of connection and inspiration.

Annie, like my mother and father, had travelled to England from Saint Vincent, and like my mother had become a nurse in this country. She had even lived for a time in my hometown of Luton, where my parents raised our family.

Annie came to England in 1861, nearly a century before my parents and others from across the Commonwealth travelled to breathe life into the still young NHS, London Transport, British Rail and other institutions hungry for young, educated labour. Annie began work as a probationer nurse at The London Hospital (now The Royal London) in 1881. Her time at The London Hospital overlapped with the four years from 1886 that Joseph Merrick, known as the 'Elephant Man', spent there in his last years after his time on the road as a freakshow attraction. Merrick's remains were interred at the City of London cemetery like Annie's, but not his skeleton, which was put on display at the hospital.

Annie was born in Saint Vincent in 1858, and her father was a Black merchant of Barbadian birth called Pharour Chaderton Brewster. Sometime in the 1860s, Pharour was widowed, and after marrying again, he brought Annie aged twelve, her sister Laura and his wife Mary, the girls' stepmother, to live in England. When the family boarded initially in Luton, they were tenants of a farmer whose widowed daughter Pharour would later marry in London after Mary had passed away. The family moved to Southwark in South London, and in 1881, aged twenty-three, Annie began her training as a nurse. She went on to give many years of service, becoming much loved, especially for her work with elderly patients with eye problems.

In 1893, Annie's father, sister and stepmother moved again when they all travelled to the United States. But Annie stayed in England and at The London Hospital. She worked there for over twenty years until she passed away unexpectedly on the morning of Tuesday, 11 February 1902 on the hospital's Victor ward, four days after what was meant to be a routine operation to remove 'a large fibroid', not thought to be malignant. The cause of death was recorded as unclear, although it is possible that it was due to peritonitis.

In 2021, wanting to find out more about Annie, I visited the Saint Bartholomew's Hospital Museum to read through archives and records from The Royal London Hospital that were held there. I spent several hours in a small, neat reading room which itself dated back to the 1730s. The skilled and diligent archivists had already kindly retrieved for me several heavy volumes of training registers and thick, dark-green-bound ward records with wide, brown spines, pages crowded with lines of text. They had been brought out in anonymous cardboard boxes filling several trays of two trollies.

I struggled to read the tight, meticulous handwriting but knew that stories and secrets were buried under the terse commentaries and bald dates and facts. When I read the contemporaneous words from her matron and colleagues about Annie's nursing career, her life and character came alive to me.

The entry in the Register of Sisters and Nurses noting Annie's death on 11 February 1902 *after 20 years faithful and devoted service* said:

> *Annie Brewster, best known to all her Hospital friends*
> *as 'Nurse Ophthalmic', spent the best and happiest years*

*of her life at the London Hospital... With her quick
intelligence she became very skilful in the treatment of
eyes, and her kindness to the poor old people who passed
through her hands during this period was unwearied.
Hospital friends mourn her loss and keep her in affection-
ate remembrance.*

That record also showed Annie's progress through promotions
and responsibility for different wards:

*Nurse Guernsey – March 25th, 1884
Nurse Charrington – Nov 2nd, 1886
Promoted on April 8th, 1888, as Ophthalmic Nurse*

However, the 1881 December register of probationers stated
that early in her training, her matron Eva Lückes noted that
Annie did not pass her nursing examination, apparently because
of her 'lamentably poor education' rather than any ignorance
of nursing. But somehow Annie seemed to have overcome that
judgement – the register also said that she was:

*... a thoroughly satisfactory probationer ... quick, thor-
ough and active. She was a favourite with all the sisters
under whom she worked ... and equally well suited for
medical and surgical work. She was gentle and kind to
her patients and showed a 'head' for managing her ward.*

Annie received a certificate to the effect that her work was
excellent and her conduct very good. She gained the title of Nurse

Ophthalmic, and the way this was used was not just a designation of the ward she was responsible for but also an expression of the respect and deep affection conferred on Annie by her colleagues. Despite the earlier judgement about her level of education, an expansive letter with her name against it appeared in the *London Daily News* in August 1890, defending the hospital against accusations that nurses were treated to harsh discipline and inadequate consideration of their welfare, with poor meals and unduly onerous tasks. Annie was a fierce defender of the necessary rigour of the nursing profession and also staunchly testified that she and her colleagues were well taken care of and supported.

When Annie passed away, the weekly summary report for Victor ward read:

> *Poor Nurse Ophthalmic, who seemed to be getting on so well after her operation (though it was a very big one), got suddenly worse on Tuesday morning and died quite unexpectedly…*

> *Unfortunately poor Nurse Ophthalmic did not make her will, though she told Matron that she would do so before her operation. Matron saw that she has no relations in England, but there is no doubt that her father will come over from New York as there are some £700 or £800 for him.*

I do not know if Annie's father made it to England to attend her burial in East London. Her death notice in the *London*

Hospital Gazette contained a black-and-white photograph of her: composed and dignified; looking out to the side of the camera view; short, dark hair just escaping her nurse's cap. Her skirt and pinafore are shaded white, covering a light grey shirt, with white cuffs and a clasp at her neck. In the photograph, her hand rests on the back of a wooden chair, and when I saw it, I thought there was sadness in her face as well as preparedness.

I looked at Annie's image and wondered if she had been lonely living in a big city far away from the Caribbean island where she had grown up. I thought about what might have sustained her after that long journey to keep training and serving, especially when her father, sister and stepmother were no longer there to come home to each evening and to tell her they were proud of her. Instead, when she opened the door to her room as she came back from the Ophthalmic ward, all she would have heard would have been the disinterested chatter and shouts of the other nurses on the dormitories in the nurses' quarters, with no connection to where she had come from.

In the West Indies, my mother and father had begun adult-hood with different dreams. My father had wanted to be an architect, and my mother initially trained in the Caribbean as a teacher. Perhaps like them, Annie, in coming to England, had to pursue different plans and ambitions. However, in their new home, all three Vincentians threw themselves into making new lives and a success of their journeys.

Annie became a trained Black professional nurse in England generations before the NHS was created and during a time that was usually looked back on without recognising the history and contribution of Britain's Black community before the twentieth century. Even before she passed away at the early age of forty-three, she was an inspiration, although what I had read about her hardworking diligence made me think that, just like my mother, she would have been unenthusiastic about being the centre of anyone's attention.

Annie helped people who could not see or who needed help to see. I came late to her story, but my mind was already opening to the stories of Vincentians like her who endured so deeply, travelled so far and left so much for the world to cherish and learn from. I was far from the first to leave the island and to travel the world trying to find it again. What bonded us all was where we had come from.

In Aotearoa New Zealand, Māori people taught me a mantra for descent, belonging, identity and connection for those who have journeyed far from where their ancestors' lives began. For me, fiery La Soufrière was the volcanic heart of the island Annie and my parents came from. Hairouna, Yurumein and Saint Vincent are all the names it has been known by, and our oceans were both the Caribbean, whose warmth lapped the leeward coast, and the wild Atlantic, whose wild waves pounded the black sands of the windward coasts near which both my mother and father were born.

After my own return to Saint Vincent, I discovered the stories of others from the island who had also been carried across the ocean and away from the arms of their families and loved ones.

Names in dusty faded pages, etched into marble, lives buried in handwritten records and shipping manifests. Their stories might have been lost for years, decades or centuries, but I wanted to uncover them and to bring them home as well.

Departures

As I grew up, I never really knew where to tell people I was from. I was born in London but raised in Luton, a medium-sized town whose economy was dominated by the (then) huge car manufacturer Vauxhall. The sprawling factory lay just off the M1 motorway at the southern entrance to the town, its yawning lawns of concrete waiting to be filled by shiny, new vehicles. The company's thirst for labour and the growth of the town tempted thousands of couples like my parents out of London in the 1960s and '70s. They came for jobs on the production line, like my father, or to support the increasing population in other ways like my mother, who was a nurse at the local hospital. With their jobs, our family could have a house with a garden and eventually a TV and a car. Like the journey to England from the Caribbean made by my parents, moving to Luton gave us opportunity.

As a boy born to parents from the West Indies, I always felt connected to my Black heritage, mainly because of our Sundays. The mornings were spent at the local Methodist church, where the slowly dwindling body of white congregants was boosted and enfolded by the new arrivals from a warmer place, singing more loudly and smiling openly and widely. On Sunday afternoons, my sister, brother and I would sneak into the immaculate front room of our house to sit on the floor between the sofa and armchairs and listen to my mother and father's friends fill it with happy voices and reggae.

On the weekends when visitors were not coming to us, we squeezed into the family car (always a Vauxhall) to visit relatives and other Vincentians who had also found places to raise and reunite their families after arriving in the UK. We drove to London suburbs like Enfield and Tottenham, and often to other towns which orbited London such as Reading and High Wycombe, a town whose name I did not know how to spell but whose two words my child's mind fused into a joyful cadence: *Hiweeecum!*

In my early years, the Caribbean enfolded me in other ways too. My father first took me 'home' when I was seven; I remember the dizzy excitement of the small boy who couldn't sleep a wink in the whole week before his first plane journey. Planes were not unfamiliar or exotic modes of transport for my parents, nor a way to carry us all to package holidays in Europe. They were just vehicles, a functional way to get home like the shuttle buses which took them to the departure gate or, at the other end of our flight, the convoy of relatives' cars that would always drive down to the airport at Arnos Vale to carry them back to Biabou.

Before my first trip to Saint Vincent, my weary class teacher had to call my father into school to try to calm my unending peaks of distraction and hyperactivity. All I recall of the journey is a moment standing transfixed on the airport concourse in Antigua – where we were changing planes to fly on to Saint Vincent – staring at the huge, pinned swordfish that leapt its

way across a wall high above, flying all by itself as it tried to
return to the sea.

In 1994, my mother and father moved back to the Caribbean,
leaving us in the cold while they retired to the house they had
saved up to build over a period of more than thirty years in
England. We gathered at an airport again, but this time roles
had been reversed. My sister Alison, brother Anthony and I
watched our parents' figures disappear in the burgeoning streams
of humanity which merged and flowed through the security
channels. My dad's flat cap, of which he was very proud, floated
along on the surface of the tide of bodies, and my mother's pink
coat bobbed within it.

Instead of offspring travelling and leaving tearful parents
behind, now it was us who would have to anchor memory and
history in England and wait for phone calls from across time
zones – Luton dinnertime colliding with Saint Vincent lunch,
London afternoons greeting Caribbean mornings. We would
have to arrange the shipping of barrels filled with clothes and gifts
and British foodstuffs for our loved ones and for the extended
family who watched over them.

Alison, Anthony and I left the terminal, dispersing to our
various car parks and the train station. As I unlocked my car,
a grey-suited, white man, running and out of breath, appeared
at the top of a staircase by the pay-for-parking machines. He
surveyed the ranks of cars and then his gaze rested on me, the
walkie-talkie in his hand crackling and snickering.

'Hey, have you been inside the terminal?'

'Yes, I was. Of course I was. I was just seeing my parents off. Why?'

'Oh. Because we had a report of someone who looks like you trying car doors.'

'Well it wasn't me, mate,' I replied, frustration and an edge in my voice.

'Right. Okay then.'

He paused and we looked at each other for what seemed to be a long time, unsure of what to make of this encounter or what to do next. Then the walkie-talkie muttered to him again and he was gone, bounding back up the stairs to the next floor.

Before my parents' plane could have reached the clouds, I had left the airport slip roads, dispersing into the circle of traffic on the M25 to head back to Luton.

Once back in Leagrave, I went upstairs to the sunlit front bedroom of the modest three-bedroomed, semi-detached house which had seemed like a palace when we moved there ten years before, with its apple tree in the garden and the front door porch for houseplants and visitors' shoes. I was tired and simply wanted to lie down.

As a child, I used to lie on my mum and dad's bed and doze near my mother as she did her weekly ironing. Why I went to their room I did not know, but watching that domestic ritual would always bring me calm and peace. That was my memory. But when I went into their room on that wintery January morning, I lay on the bed and this time I did not stay on top of the covers but pulled the red-and-white polyester covering with its large floral blooms over me. Sunlight streamed through the window, but although I could see a pile of clothes on a chair and the ironing board was still there, the bedroom felt cold and hideously empty. I twisted my head into the pink cotton pillowcase and wept.

Bertie

July 1922, Shirley, Southampton

Bertie was dreaming again. He stood on a hill which overlooked the port of Kingstown and stared at the mail steamer moored in the bay below. Out in the distance, Bequia, Battowia and Balliceaux floated like surfaced whales basking in a flat sea. A separate part of his mind wondered how he knew the names of those islands, because there was certainly a time when he did not. But that was before he began service at Harewood House. A place where in quiet moments between his duties he would steal away to a room containing a globe almost as tall as himself and slowly spin it, his finger flying across painted seas and continents and tracing over the smallest dots as he tried to find where he had come from.

In his dream, the wind carried the men's curses clearly as they shuttled barrels and trunks from shore to deck, although the words made no sense to him. Bearded, burly white men who hurled large bundles of mail onto a boat as if they were the bags of coal he had seen tossed into the cellars at Harewood House. He wondered if he would see Harewood again and walk the wide corridors beneath the unsmiling portraits of lords and ladies. Whether he would ever return and enter fine drawing rooms so large that a young boy could escape to lie beneath a table, slowly reading letters spotted with the tears of his mummy, her love set out in handwriting that was not her own.

He dreamt of that one time he had gone home again. His mother and father, Emilia and William, stood beside him, tall in the clothes they wore to vend their goods at market, respectable enough for town but well-worn and many times patched and darned. Bertie was dressed much more smartly in clothes finer even than those that his parents kept safe and clean to dress the children in on Sunday. On that Kingstown hill there was no one to serve, but still he wore formal black trousers and his Harewood navy-blue serving jacket with yellow beading and buttons emblazoned with a heraldic muzzled bear.

It already seemed to him that his mother and father's skin was burnt a deeper black than his, their lines and wrinkles earnt selling their provisions under the hot sun in the crowded streets down by the port. Their wooden cart crammed with plantain, banana, arrowroot and cassava as they competed with the shouts and wares of the other Middle Street vendors nearby. His family, unless sleeping, were constantly exposed to the sun.

When he came back that one time to visit, they listened with wide eyes as he described his thirteen years within the sheltered splendour of Harewood House as pageboy and footman, and how he always had the shelter of umbrellas and carriages to protect him from the Yorkshire autumn rain or the cold snow and harsh winters.

Mummy had a bundle of food for him in her hand, bundled in red cloth. In his dream, his three brothers and his sisters were there too, although that confused him because he knew from his mother's letters that Ormond, his youngest brother, had passed away just four years after Bertie had left the island.

His mother and father still had several mouths to feed even after he had been taken away. His mother sent many letters to Yorkshire asking for help, and the regular remittances and gifts of clothes he had grown out of started coming back to the island from England. But still his mother had cried when the Lascelles brought him back, although so much of the family's support depended on him being away. Now she was crying as he got ready to leave again – this time by his own choice because he did not want to stay on this small island when he knew the world was so much bigger.

'Egbert stay nah. We ah go manage. We nah need the money. We need you. Mi need you.'

He wanted to answer, but the words could not escape his mouth. He could breathe, but he did not know if the tightness in his chest came from the jacket binding him in or from some other feeling.

'Bertie,' said an English voice behind him, 'we have to go now.'

When he woke, his sleep and dreams had been disturbed, perhaps by a horse and dray trundling down the road towards the port.

Bertie rolled over and away from the quietly breathing shape beside him, still covered by the thin sheet he had had to throw off. The breeze from the open window played across his face, the fluttering curtains and nets letting in light and glimpses of the blue sky and the terraced houses on the other side of the road. Already it was too hot in the room, even though in dawn's half-light he had padded over to the window to pull the frame up and let in air. He had slept again till he could hear the loud trill of the street sparrows, and when he opened his eyes, he felt sure that everything was going to sort out. The woman who shared the lodging with him was still half asleep but turned to wrap her arms around him, and it was then that he heard the knock at the door.

Outside, an elderly Black man had opened his front door and, without stepping onto the path, leant round the corner and over the low brick wall to rap the knocker of the house next door again. It was mid-afternoon, and Rodgers could see the net curtains stirring with the slight breeze through the half-open, first-floor windows – it was a stifling day. But he heard no response or shifting from within, so he knocked for a third time, this time calling out.

'Egbert! Egbert! Boy, get up nah! Mi know yuh ah dey!'

Now he heard movement and then the sound of footsteps coming down a wooden-floored passageway like the one he had in his own house. The door opened, and Bertie bounced out onto the mosaic of the pathway barefoot, a white shirt flapping loosely over his trousers. He was smiling, his face still boyishly handsome although he was in his forties. His hair held a meticulously straight parting down the left side, although from his state of dress he had clearly not been up long.

'Morning, Mr Rodgers!' Bertie said breezily, his words holding an almost affected formality, and yet behind them was a faint Northern accent.

'Morning? Boy, it not morning – de clock pass noon long time!'

'Ah, but it is my morning, Mr Rodgers.'

Rodgers sucked his teeth. In the few days he had known the new lodger next door, he had come to realise that the younger man chatted plenty and most of it was foolishness.

'Listen, boy, mi nah come to play with you. You wan' some work?'

'Work, Mr Rodgers?'

'Work yes! You remember wha' dat is?'

Now Bertie straightened up from where he had been leaning on the wall and the smile disappeared from his face.

'Mr Rodgers, nah speak to mi so. I work hard since I was a chile. Mi mammy nah raise no lazy pickney. I work for some of the finest people in this land, and dey treat mi like one of dem own. Lords and ladies, Mr Rodgers.' Now that he was speaking for longer and was not holding a pose, Egbert's tones came closer to the same Caribbean lilt that Rodgers spoke with.

'One of dem own…' Rodgers shook his head and sucked his teeth again. 'Boy, as long as yuh skin stay dat colour, yuh could never be one ah dem.'

'Yuh don't know how it was, Mr Rodgers. I use to work in a big, big house. Big as a castle up in Yorkshire. I travel far and wide. Dem take me everywhere. And I tek care of mi family back home in Saint Vincent too. I always mek sure to sen' something back for dem.'

'Alright, alright, alright. Mi tired hear about dis big, fancy house and all yuh fine clothes and everyt'ing. Why yuh nah there now? Seem like yuh fall 'pon hard times to mi.'

Bertie did not reply straight away, and when he did, his voice was very quiet.

'Mi lan' in a likkle piece of trouble. Mi borrow some money and dem call de police 'pon mi.'

'Yuh borrow dis money?'

'Alright then! Mi tek it. But was for a fren'.'

'Oh Lawd, boy, wha' mek yuh so stupid? Nah badder push up yuh face at mi. Ah who dis fren'?'

'Her name is Elizabeth, Mr Rodgers.'

Rodgers stared at him and again sucked his teeth loudly. 'Mi should ah know it gwan be a gal. And where dis fren' now?'

'Mr Rodgers, nah talk so 'bout her. She is beautiful. She is in Yorkshire, Mr Rodgers, and have mi baby. He is one year old.'

Rodgers stared at him but knew not to press too hard. 'Ah wha' yuh ah go do now?'

'I'm leaving, Mr Rodgers. Mi need some work.'

'Leaving? Leaving fah where? Yuh only just arrive. Mi know someone have some work for yuh at de pub.'

'No, Mr Rodgers, mi hafi leave dis country. Mi nah trus' what might happen if mi stay. De Earl of Harewood tell mi to get out of dis country or he gwan mek sure mi go to prison. Mi just ah res' up here for a few weeks.'

'What about de chile and 'im mother?'

'Mr Rodgers, mi ah come back for dem. I jus' need to let t'ings calm down and get meself fix up. I coming back, I promise.'

'So wey yuh ah go?'

'Trinidad, Mr Rodgers.'

'Trinidad! Boy, what the arse yuh talkin' 'bout? Trinidad! Wha' yuh know about Trinidad?'

'Mi meet a man and 'im promise me some work out there. He help mi get a ticket. De boat sail on the twenty-ninth from Dover.'

Rodgers was left without words. He waited a long time before he spoke again, and while they stood in the sunshine, three hoots of a steamship's horn sounded from the nearby docks.

'Egbert…'

'*Call mi Bertie, Mr Rodgers. Yuh and I is friends now.*'

'*Bertie. Dis not a bad place for a Black man, yuh know. Dey is a lot of we here from a long time. People here, you know, was among dem who fight slavery the hardest. White people. Dey even help some ah dem slaves from Africa return home. Yuh see de statue over dey?*'

Bertie let his gaze follow that of the old man along the line of the brick wall and to the plinth that separated the gates of the two houses, where an intricately carved stone pineapple stood.

'*Yuh know what that means? Dat dis ah a place of welcome. This town ah full of dem. Dem say it was the sea captains who brought that sign here, but it go back all the way to the islands an' to our people. Bertie, dis ah a good place to stop. T'ings will sort out.*'

'*Mr Rodgers, de ticket done book. On de* Van Rensselaer.'

'*Boy, yuh trust a ship fah carry yuh so far? Yuh nah hear dem six hundred South African soldiers sink 'pon de Mendi?*'

'*Mr Rodgers, dat was wartime. Dat ship get ram. T'ings different now. I already travel back home once, and dis is a Dutch ship mi ah tek. Everything gwan be fine.*'

'*Yuh mind mek up?*'

'*Mr Rodgers, yes. But watch. Yuh ah go see mi again. Alyuh ah go hear mi name again. How mi ah go leave mi chile and nah come back?*'

The ship's horn sounded again, and this time both men stayed silent as the blasts faded across the city.

Part II

NORTHLAND AND BIABOU

Lin

September 1974, Fort Worth

Lin sits in her room in the nurses' quarters reading a letter from Winston. She is feeling happy because one arrived yesterday as well – she tries to write to him nearly every single day, and it lifts her mood so much when he does the same. On any morning that she recognises the curves of his handwriting on the outside of one of the letters stuffed into her pigeonhole, joy bubbles up inside her. It is all she can do to resist finding ways to sneak off the wards and get away from her bustling Texan colleagues to read it. But she does not want to risk any disapproval, not when so much for her family rides on her success out here. So she waits until she can get back to her room and she can be alone with Win and his words.

Later that day, she writes in her small diary that both letters are 'loving and cheerful' because arrangements are progressing well for Win to be able to come over. The estate agents have come up with a good valuation for the house in Luton and there is plenty of interest already. Their new life in the States can begin soon, with them and the children reunited.

Through her bedroom door she can hear the clatter of plates in the kitchen – it is Nema, the Sri Lankan nurse who shares the apartment they live in. Both of them speak excellent English, but they are shy and strangers in a strange land, so for now most of their communication is through smiles and the meals they share, introducing each other to the foods of the islands where they were born. A long time ago, when she first set sail for England, her mother had told her 'always travel with your conscience and your appetite'. So Lin tried new foods with gusto, from the huge burgers and fries she struggled to get through in the shopping-mall franchises to the delicious chicken curry with rice and pol sambol that Nema would prepare after they had finished their shifts.

There is no chair or table in her bedroom so she perches on the edge of the bed, but she constantly has to move – the mattress seems to be filled only with springs.

There is another letter beside her, unopened – blue with a stamp filled with red hibiscus flowers. This one is from Saint Vincent, but the sender's name tells her it is not from the children, and she thinks it will be one asking for more money.

As she shifts to get comfortable, the packages beside her roll across the thin blanket. She is gathering things to send down for the children, and with the presents, candies and clothes she will include an envelope of money for the people looking after them, and American food tins, batteries and candles. The children's gifts are for Christmas: a small red radio for her eldest son; ribbons and a doll for the girl (one with a white complexion was all she could find downtown); a ball and puzzles for the little boy. Still to be wrapped up and added is a big, salted ham for the children's carers to supplement their household's supplies for the festive period.

Outside, taxi horns blare and small children shrivel in the Texan heat. Soon she will have to hurry. Her next shift starts in an hour, and she does not know how to smooth over any late arrival by making small talk with the people she works with. The other nurses still remark on the contrast – to them – of her British accent and the dark colour of her skin, but serious teasing rarely happens. But she notices that they are slow to trust her with any of the more senior tasks on the wards or to give her the responsibility of summarising the women's medical histories and complications to the doctors.

It is a while before she opens and reads the letter with the hibiscus flowers stamp and the words sealed inside the aerogramme reach her eyes. The letter is from the woman who, together with her husband, is meant to be taking care of Lin's three children. She wants to tell Lin more about how they are being treated. She did not want to worry Lin with a phone call but… there were things that she thought that perhaps Lin was not aware of and that might make her want to come for them sooner than planned. Or perhaps to ask one of Lin's sisters to come down from Dickson and fetch them.

As the realisation of what has happened to her children sinks into Lin, tears seep from her eyes and stream down her face. They come in response to the children's sobs she can now hear in her mind, borne on hurricane winds rising from the Caribbean. The three of them parentless when she should be with them, while she tends infants whose mothers have Southern drawls, stepping around their blonde, tanned husbands who fill all the space they can and look down to hide their proud grins under Stetsons and baseball caps.

She reads the letter again and wonders what she should do. She remembers holding them, all three, in her arms at Heathrow and trying to comfort them.

'I soon coming for you. Just be good for Mummy and Daddy and very soon we all ah go be back together like a family again.'

Just before they were taken through the departure gate by the passenger assistance lady, her eldest screamed, 'Why, Mummy? Why, Mummy? Why, why?'

Before that day, there had been many late nights sitting up with Winston in the kitchen in Luton, talking and planning and browsing shiny brochures. Weighing up many facts and figures. They had filled in and despatched endless forms. But still when her child asked, 'Why, Mummy?' she could not find an answer for him.

Nema tapped at the door. 'Lin! Dinner's ready.'

She had to eat, and it was nearly time to go back to the ward. She let her hand rest briefly again on the packages and left the room, leaving the task of wrapping to await her return.

Arrivals

Before and after university I did not have the resources to take a gap year, and I could not afford to go backpacking. But after some years working with the Deaf community in Bedfordshire and for an organisation led by disabled people in London, I wanted an adventure and to see more of the world.

In the early 1990s, I began considering my options – I had a social work qualification and degree, and experience of providing support in the community to Deaf and disabled people. The only spoken language I was proficient in was English, and because I would have to work and earn money, I needed to go somewhere where my social work qualification would be recognised. But I wanted to travel to a place that was different in other ways and where I could come into contact with new cultures.

I had spoken about my desire to travel with a hugely inspirational lecturer called Murray Ryburn from Aotearoa, who taught me on my social work course at the University of Birmingham. In classes and tutorials, Murray spoke about the social and community work innovations to address inequality, injustice and social exclusion that were being tried or developed in Aotearoa: welfare and housing safety nets and recognising the power and place of cultural practices and tribal relationships for indigenous people through family group conferences.

I listened raptly to Murray when he shared these perspectives. I thought that in Aotearoa I might find some sort of Scandinavian-style social welfare bohemia, even though months after I arrived in the country, friends would tell me that many of the programmes that had inspired me had already been rolled back. As an eager and idealistic newly qualified social worker, Aotearoa sounded like a wonderful place to both develop my practice and to encounter new worlds, even though some people told me I would not enjoy it there. They worried that after living in London I might find Aotearoa too quiet or that I would be lonely and isolated there as a Black man. But still I chose to go because I wanted to explore the world.

I sent letters and emails to many organisations, conscious – despite the initial lack of replies – that all I needed was one positive response. Eventually I received it, and after a telephone interview, the Deaf Association of New Zealand invited me to come and work as a service co-ordinator supporting the local Deaf community from one of their regional offices.

In 1995, my parents, brother and sister, now joined by my girlfriend, gathered again at Heathrow. This time it was not for a flight heading to the Caribbean but to farewell me as I set off to the Southern Hemisphere. We hugged and kissed, and then I filed through the banded aisles leading to Security. When I got to the other side of an anonymous grey screen which separated two worlds, I set down my hand luggage and leant against it, crying floods of tears, overcome by the enormity of leaving everything familiar to me. Against that wall, my sports bag between my legs, I regressed again to my small-boy self – heartbroken, alone and lost in the vastness of an airport terminal.

When I arrived in Aotearoa a few days later after a stopover in Hong Kong, I was immediately exposed to forces and currents that I had never before in my life experienced. As the plane flew in low over the hills surrounding Auckland, I marvelled at the beauty of the uneven volcanic hills, like pool balls that had been hidden under the green baize instead of being placed on top of it. My new manager, Lynda, picked me up from Auckland Airport, and en route to the family I was to stay with initially, we called in at a Māori cultural competition being held in the South Auckland suburbs.

'We'll just pop in,' Lynda said, but it was hours before we emerged again, my jetlagged eyes unable even to blink into the sunlight.

The unassuming sports hall was packed with what was probably only hundreds of people, but it seemed like thousands because of the noise they made. The audience was made up of Māori families mostly, adults and children cheering and whooping for their favourites. The performers represented who they were and where they were from, their home places and their bonds. For everyone in that hall, except possibly me, this occasion was a celebration of culture and connection.

This was not an event that would be on any tourist itinerary, and I knew I should have felt privileged watching the competitors perform vibrant and energetic haka and dances in traditional dress, but my tiredness was overwhelming. My eyes fought to stay open through jetlag and exhaustion, and I struggled to take in what should have been the excitement of being present in the crowd. After the flight, I had little energy left to me to reflect on how fortunate I was to be witnessing these performances only a few hours after I had arrived in the country.

Memories are like hand luggage when you are travelling, and sometimes it takes a while before you can unpack them. Mine had to stay bundled up for three days spent in long stretches of jetlagged sleep while outside the rain fell from leaden skies. I wrote home to my family in England that the rain in Aotearoa never hung around for long, but when I arrived, the clouds seemed fixed in place as if to give me a reminder of what I had left behind and to make my transition from the UK less jarring.

The days when I was more awake passed in a whir of induction, paperwork, initial training and meeting new colleagues at the Deaf Association of New Zealand. But although the skies cleared, and I quickly grew to like Auckland with its bays and beaches and the friendly welcome of the new people I met, my travelling was not over. Auckland was just another waypoint on my journey across hemispheres.

The Deaf Association's regional services were spread across the whole country – a network of small offices mostly served by one or two people and working with Deaf and deafened people across cities, towns and remote rural locations. My destination was Northland – Te Tai Tokerau – the part of the country pointing north towards the Equator. Back in England, as I pored over my shiny new edition of the *Lonely Planet* guidebook, I had seized on the fact that the climate was described as semi-subtropical.

I was to be based in the biggest regional settlement and Aotearoa's northernmost city, Whangārei. I arrived to a traditional welcome of a Māori *pōwhiri*. A group of local Deaf people congregated outside the centre where the Deaf Association local office was based, and they shared songs and speeches to welcome me to their community and their land. I could never have imagined how moving the songs and speeches would be in three languages: New Zealand Sign Language, Māori and English. Both Deaf and Māori culture and pride were richly expressed and introduced to me.

On the drive up to Whangārei, my area manager Allan had prepared me for what to expect and explained that we should offer a song too as part of my reception ceremony. He had come with a suggestion, and as we drove northwards, I practised and practised to try to memorise 'United We Stand', but I still struggled to remember the English lyrics when we gave our contribution. For some reason, I felt more at ease when we all joined in a *waiata* sung in Māori, reading the words from a printed script, my heart already joining in with the sentiments:

Ehara i te mea
Nō ināianei te aroha
Nō nga tūpuna

Tuku iho, tuku iho
Not the thing
of recent times, is love
but by the ancestors it has been
passed down, passed down.

I started work immediately, but my letters home were mostly full of what I was doing with my time off. Northland was a wonderland for me, its steamy warmth a delight after the squalls, drizzle and grey clouds of Auckland. I was constantly exploring, always finding out more.

This is how weekend afternoons were at the beginning of my time in Northland. I might drive south of Whangārei, along the coast of the harbour which on the map the city perched at the top of, and walk around Bream Head, trying to find the location of an ancient Māori *pā* site indicated on my Department of Conservation map. I was never actually sure that I found the right place. I would tramp in the bush in transient gloom and showers, crossing bridges which to me seemed straight out of an Indiana Jones movie in their wobbliness, shredding my nerves.

Usually I explored on my own, and often wherever I went I found myself utterly alone. It was a different me doing this exploring from the person who had occupied the same skin only months before. I had no idea why I didn't feel anxious to be out there on my own, but I wasn't even worried when I slid down a slope in the mud, feeling a momentary but dizzying loss of control, or got lost in dense forest, unable to find any feature to orient my damp and creased tourist map by.

I learnt to take more heed of the directions for walkers, which if they said a hike would take two hours really did mean that, no matter how fit I thought I was. Here there was no nannying bureaucracy to ensure netting was there to save me from plunging over an unguarded cliff edge, to remind me more than once to dress appropriately in case of bad weather or to plant a path of signs to lead me out of the bush if I did not take a compass.

From what I saw in news reports, peril – in boats at sea or on lakes, paragliding in the air, hiking in the mountains and in the bush – was never far away and was accepted. Far away from where I had grown up, I now had to be entirely responsible for my actions and decisions. I remember feeling dislocated and lonely, but never scared.

When my day's adventures were done, I would return to my little flat in Whangārei feeling muddy, manly and tired. At home in those days, when I had no friends, entertainment meant revelling in the TV's supply of *The Simpsons* and National Provincial Championship rugby. I was on my own. There was no one near who knew me well, no one to run to, and initially I felt deeply that I left no mark in this society, as if I were lost and alone in the bush at Bream Head.

Gradually and slowly, I made friends who joined me on my journeys. My co-workers Margie and Alex, who were both Māori, shared with me their knowledge and awareness of the needs of the local Deaf community, and brought me into the warm welcome of their own families and homes. I began watching the Auckland Warriors Rugby League team on Friday nights inspired by Alex's example – he had no time for the overpowered fripperies of rugby union. Before finding a flat of my own, I lodged with Margie's mum Teresa, and we shared meals and nights in front of the TV as she asked me about England and where my family had come from. I found it easier to talk with Teresa about all the parts of my life than I did with many people in England.

For Deaf Awareness Week, we supported local people to deliver a workshop called 'Signs of Life' to increase awareness of the Deaf community. The local newspaper, *The Northern Advocate*, profiled our service with a photograph of Alex and me – two tall, hearing men of colour – strolling casually along the street, our relaxed, staged conversation used to increase awareness of a culture neither of us had been born into.

I found aspects of Northland that were not described in my guidebook, and my friends Rose and Natalee became companions for my weekend explorations there and further afield. Rose took me to Rotorua and the Coromandel, where I paddled in hot springs, and Natalee and I drove to Cape Reinga at the very tip of the North Island, which in Māori lore was the departure point of the spirits. There, beguiled, I watched the waves clash as two seas met and tussled with each other.

The creativity and artistry of individuals was everywhere too, in the little pop-up exhibitions of paintings or pottery in every small town and beach community, appearing when I least expected it. When we drove through the forests of the Far North

District and our map confused us, a fairy-tale round house made entirely of wood breathed quietly and waited for us to find it, watching us draw closer through a deep encasement of trees. If buildings had souls and could smile, that one did as it saw our faces transform with amazement and pleasure at the ingenuity of its creation, the same reaction shown by other lost travellers who came that way.

I travelled to see the famous and fabled giant kauri in the Waipoua Forest. On the boardwalk through the forest, dense vegetation and ferns thrust up either side of me, the path falling and rising like a wooden wave through the ferns and other foliage. All around was a bewildering blur of green until a wall emerged from the indistinct shapes of the forest ahead. I wondered why someone would erect and leave a wall at the end of a wooden path in the middle of nowhere. But then I realised that this was a colossal tree – Tāne Mahuta, more than 2,000 years old – that stretched the arc of my eyesight even though I was standing fully twenty metres way. The colossal size of the tree had been impossible to imagine. I was made insignificant by its size, and it was ridiculous to think that even five versions of me with outstretched arms could come close to girdling this God of the Forest.

There were many other expeditions and wonders discovered: Ninety-Mile Beach (not ninety miles long but still never-ending) and the hulk of the Rainbow Warrior. The festivals against French nuclear proliferation in small towns dotted along the coast. With

Rose, I walked along beaches which owed comparison to nothing else in this world but in their blue waters and golden beaches took me back to the Caribbean and long-ago memories of a time in childhood – a time when I was in Saint Vincent and my favourite T-shirt (one given me by my beloved Uncle Cluston) had a picture of a little boy chilling by the sea, his sunglasses askew, frowning with feigned annoyance, and beneath him the words 'I Got Sand In My Shoes'.

On a work assignment, I accompanied a young man to view a state house that he might possibly be allocated. It was a modest bungalow in a quiet, working-class suburb, but while he slowly walked around the empty rooms, he ummed and aahed, asking in sign language what I thought about various aspects.

I stared at the lemon tree in the middle of the generous grassy backyard. It reminded me of the apple tree in my mum and dad's garden back in Luton, but this young man would live on his own and his bungalow would not be hemmed in so that he needed a passage to get to the back yard. That was my first understanding that the expectations and possibilities of land here on the other side of the world could be so different from the crowded terraces and handkerchief gardens of London and Luton. It became clear that I had a lot to adapt to and that I had to see with different eyes too.

I had travelled 10,000 miles to end up in Whangārei. But my cultural dislocation felt way more significant than my physical one. I saw people with brown skin like me on the news routinely in a way that was unfamiliar. I saw them as programme anchors and commentators, not as isolated outrider or 'outstanding' individuals, and they were presenting the news not just the subject and focus of bulletins about famine, crime, riots or poverty. For me it was inspiring and refreshing to see how interwoven Māori culture was with the mainstream of the country's politics and culture.

As an outsider, I felt that I had little right to overanalyse the dynamics of race and history in Aotearoa and that I should observe respectfully. But from the start it had a profound impact on me. I knew that I should not be too romantic, wide-eyed or idealistic. Just like ethnic minority communities in the UK, I had seen that Māori and Pacific Islander people were statistically more likely to be out of employment, face significant health challenges or come into contact with the criminal justice system. But I also saw a degree of commitment to enabling their representation, respect and self-determination that to me was unexpected and inspiring.

I was particularly struck by the debate about land ownership. Unlike the situation that I understood existed in Australia, it seemed that the conversation was not about whether any land should be returned to the first settlers of Aotearoa – that was taken as a given, a right and a correction of colonial injustice. The debates were about *how much* land. Everywhere I went I could see bi- and multi-culturalism supported in a way that did not chime with my Black British experience. I saw genuine attempts to achieve the empowerment of minority communities and the celebration of Māori language and tradition by New Zealanders of all backgrounds.

As well as the acceptance and merging of Māori, Pasifika and European influences, the country had absorbed other migrants and cultures too, and embraced the genesis of new streams of identity, such as that of Chinese Māori people.

My self-awareness had expanded in Aotearoa and had been nourished by the atmosphere of Māori kinship which surrounded me, from the rich heritage and pride in impoverished Northland communities to the strength, celebration and representation in big cities and in the media. I realised this was not the full or only story, and that not everything I thought I saw might be permanent and deep-seated. But I truly hoped it was.

Black friends in the UK had told me not to go to Aotearoa – there would be no Black people like me there, they said. But that of course was not true any more than it had been true of Britain for many centuries prior to the arrival of the Windrush generation. There were not many other people of Caribbean or African descent to be sure, and when we fellow travellers met, we watched each other keenly like cats caught on the narrow pathway of a garden fence. The Black guy I passed on the pavement of a wide, busy street in Auckland, each of us giving a small nod to the other with a half-smile before I worked up the courage to double back and ask where I might find someone who could cut my hair. The African barber in the small shop he directed me to, whose own path to Aotearoa I somehow forgot to enquire about. There was a French-speaking Rasta from New Caledonia called Patrick who I met in a coffee shop in Whangārei and who I chatted with about his islands, half a world away from the Caribbean. And the tall, lithe American basketball player who worked with youth in the South Auckland suburbs, his accent and height as alien and beguiling to me as I thought it must have been initially for those young people.

Despite these moments of connection, there were many little cultural and linguistic stumbles for me. Some made me cringe with embarrassment, like regularly forgetting the reminders of my Māori colleagues to not lean with my bottom against tables as it was considered unhygienic. But they were always kind and gentle with my inability to remember. Other incidents eventually made me smile, like the telephone call with a colleague in HR which seemed to last for interminable minutes.

'Alastair, I need to speak to someone about my pay this month.'

'Ah the old greengages then.'

'No wages, my salary – can you hear me?'

'Yes, getting your greengages, right?'

'No, Alastair – I'm asking about getting paid!'

'Yes, I know. Greengages – wages. I used to live in Stepney for a while...'

'Hah, hah,' I laughed weakly, thinking it one of the most surreal conversations I had ever had.

On another Monday morning, I shared coffee first thing with Trevor, the union official who also rented an office in the building where I worked. We exchanged pleasantries, and I told him about my latest exploits exploring the countryside. In return, he told me that at the weekend, he and his son had been tying up a bull ready to shoot it for meat. Late at night, Trevor had been woken by a huge commotion outside on the farm. Unfortunately, his son had put a slipknot in the rope when he tied up the bull. The rope had drawn tight around the bull's neck, and it was going mad as it slowly strangled itself. Trevor grabbed a long knife, meaning to cut it free, but as the animal flailed, the vicious scythes of its horns threatened to gore him. Eventually he got close enough to be inside the arc of their rake, but then he was caught as the bull's body jack-knifed against his and flung him across the yard and against the frame of a shed.

Then there was silence, except for the wheezes and rattling as the last air in the bull's lungs escaped. It had jumped into a ditch and broken its neck on the steep sides. It was still alive though, and as quickly as his aching body allowed, Trevor climbed down into the gulley and cut the heaving animal's throat with his knife. If the meat was to be recovered, the carcass needed to be gutted there and then, but he was too battered and bruised to do this, and as a result, $1,000 worth of meat went to waste.

My coffee went untasted as I listened to this story in shocked horror. This was very different from London tales of a weekend spent at a barbeque or painting the spare room.

I went on another trip to the Far North, visiting Mangonui, Cable Bay, Awanui and Kaitaia and picked up two English hitchhikers implausibly called Giles and Miles. I secretly felt smug that, although I had not seen as much of Aotearoa's two biggest islands as they had, I had been drenched in experiences simply by living and working there and had no need to be a tourist.

After dropping them off at Mangonui, I doubled back to Akatere and visited a Māori family in a small, isolated farming community. After I had completed my assessment for equipment requested by the Deaf member of the family, his father said to me, 'Hey, bro, wanna come see our land?'

We got into their car and trundled along a dusty goat track for miles, passing between the dappled hills. All of this used to belong to our *iwi* and *whanau*, they explained, but now the owners were Europeans, and it was used to grow bland pines for the forestry industry. They had filed a claim to reclaim their land with the Waitangi Tribunal, which had the task of making recommendations to the government on matters relating to the Treaty of Waitangi signed between Māori *iwi* (tribes) and the British Crown in 1840 and which included clauses asserting Māori ownership of their lands, forests and villages. Months later, the family were still waiting to find out if their claim had been successful.

We came to a beautiful beach which they told me was called Waimahana Bay, the predominant colours of gold and green rising out of shimmering blue. This was their remaining land, hidden and private. And for this family it was their abundant wealth too, not in terms of monetary value but because they were part of it, and it was part of them.

Natural wonders aside, I also found time to explore big-city life on trips back to Auckland. I caught a Mapplethorpe exhibition at the city museum, and despite the beauty of the orchids and film stars that his photographs framed, I wondered how no one else seemed to notice or care about his objectification of the Black male body. I listened to Sweet Honey in the Rock belt out 'Ain't That Good News' and other songs in the Aotea Centre, and the music made me homesick for a place I had never been to. Their powerful blend of acapella and gospel charted centuries of Black bondage, resistance, empowerment and emancipation. As Alice Walker wrote in *Anything We Love Can Be Saved*: 'These songs said: We do not come from people who have had nothing. We come, rather, from people who've had everything – except money, except political power, except freedom.' As I listened, I heard how powerful Black expression and creativity could be as a way of telling unheralded stories.

On a night out with work colleagues in Auckland, we ended up at someone's flat where I sat cross-legged on the floor drinking beer and listening to the rhythms of the room, excited and intoxicated voices fizzing around the bodies which danced to Pacific reggae. I was more than half drunk, and the cigarette smoke and dimmed lights made the space feel mystical and otherworldly. I talked with an older Māori man sitting on the sofa as he drew on a reefer and told me about his family's language (*te reo*) and culture and history (*whakapapa*), and I listened enraptured. Then he leant down to me, his voice softened by age and innumerable draws, and asked me, 'What about you?'

'What?' I said.

'Where do your people come from?'

'My mum and dad come from an island called Saint Vincent,' I told him. 'They were both born there, but they met in England.'

'Like Jamaica? They got really good weed there, bro?'

'No, it's a small island. Really small. Jamaica is much bigger.'

'You been there? Tell me about your family. What's it like there? People have a good life there, eh, bro?'

'Yes,' I said. 'I lived there. But a long while ago. I don't remember much at all.'

I felt embarrassed that I had so few answers for him. What he had asked about were all things which belonged to and were a part of me, but lately I had only sailed on their surface. I wanted to be able to share my story, but had gaps to fill in the connection with my family's history and our beautiful island cradle. It was as if I had ignored the currents and streams which had carried me to this time in my life. Embarrassed, I left and went to dance till dawn in a club on K Street.

I had loved being in Aotearoa, but after only six months I still knew very little about the country and its people. Yet it seemed to me that it was accepted that through the gaze of their children, the ancestors still looked out on the beauty of the land.

Driving back home one day after spending some time in Auckland, playing various tapes loud on the car stereo to keep me awake, the sun appeared in a gorgeous evening sky from behind storm clouds. From the speakers, Jimmy Cliff sang, 'I can see clearly now,' and suddenly I could too. As I drove through Orewa, I saw the highest point of a rainbow out to sea, peeking out above the rooftops. I pulled over and found a cliff overlooking the beach. There, nestling between the arms of land, was the rainbow's huge, beautiful and complete arc. It was the first time in my life that I had been able to see a whole rainbow, end to end, like a doorway placed there by the universe. 'Come on through,' it seemed to be saying.

My six months in Northland came to an end on another hidden beach at the end of summer. Blankets were spread on the sand, and paper plates tumbled and escaped in the light wind which caused no other bother except to the waves which it frothed. Platters of chicken and jugs full of fruit juice were shared among the guests. Banners and balloons hung down from the branches of crimson-blossomed pōhutukawa for my leaving party. The slow-moving waves lapped their way close to the base of the trees, stumbling across the sand almost as if by accident, the water an iridescent azure.

The beach that we were picnicking on, and the land we crossed before it, also belonged to Māori families, and the way down to the foreshore had been past unassuming and modest bungalows on which the paint was peeling. But regardless of what these homes looked like on the outside, I knew that they were full of human warmth within.

I shared the sunshine and food with co-workers, friends and Deaf people I had worked with while based in Whangārei. I had made connections for life: Deaf female elders – *kuia*– and their families had laughed with me, teased me for my slightly stiff English ways and taken me under their wing and into their dominions. On Māori family land at Pipiwai, I had had my first taste of inland wild swimming, bombing with my knees under my chin into a pond whose deep bottom I could not see. After being invited to a family barbecue on a hot Christmas Day, I ran through a field of endless wildflowers, and I cried with unfettered laughter alongside my workmates on an expedition to Whananaki when the trail became more goat track than road, and my car had to be lifted, not even pulled, over a ditch. I met joy and acceptance and had forgotten all my shyness.

As I was farewelled by local Māori Deaf people, I was surrounded by magic, mystery and solemnity, and I accepted the salutations of people whose culture, despite colonisation, was alive and vibrant and who honoured those lucky enough to come close to it. I was ready to visit Saint Vincent again for the first time in twenty years, suffused with this spirit of togetherness and *whanau* (family) which had surrounded me here in Aotearoa.

In the Northland settlements I visited, I had finally understood what the jargon of kinship could really mean. I saw that *whanau* was not just about relationships bound within four domestic walls but could flow outwards to support people to negotiate blocks and stumbles on the way to happiness, empowerment and well-being in the wider world.

In Aotearoa, I had come across the work of the Just Therapy Family Centre in Wellington and read about how their work with Māori and Pasifika communities did not just pay lip service to cultural and spiritual ties but was led by and informed by them. The work of the centre was focused on three core principles: *belonging* – linking to where the people who used their services came from, who their people were and what their ancestry was; *sacredness* – a spiritually focused respect and acceptance for humanity and life, acknowledging the deep link between body and soul; and *liberation* – honouring and listening to the stories of communities and individuals and through those acts finding new routes to freedom, hope and reconciliation.

My plans to return to Saint Vincent had already been set and in motion before going to Aotearoa but being in the Southern Hemisphere had invigorated and inspired *how* I was going back.

Previously I had used an exercise called 'Dreams and Goals' with some of the people who were now sitting next to me on the sand. I would sit down on the floor with the young person or Deaf adult I was working with, and instead of filling out forms or questionnaires with multiple-choice answers, we started with a big sheet of flipchart paper. The aim was to identify a path to breaking down barriers, and to do so we began by drawing the outline of a big, fluffy cloud which was to be filled with wishes and aspirations. These wishes might be to get a job or enrol on a course, to meet new friends or move out from their parents and live independently, or to travel. Now that I was getting ready to leave Aotearoa, I needed to fill my dream-cloud with my own goals.

On a final trip through the Northland countryside, I felt compelled to pull the blue Fiesta over to the side of the road. I was held and entranced by the fairy-tale view of hills and valleys stretching away into the distance. I was in an enchanted place, and I could feel the earth hum. It felt as if the spirituality of the land had entered me.

Māori people did not only introduce themselves with a name at a meeting or a gathering – they shared their tribe and genealogy, their sacred places and their links to the land, rivers and mountains. Distant voices had started calling to me and, as I planned flights and routes to the Caribbean, I ached to go to where my mother and father had been born and to grasp again the memories which had escaped me.

It was time to go home.

Islands

Two days after leaving Aotearoa in 1995, I was in the United States. I travelled to New York via Los Angeles and joined my then girlfriend to explore the city for a few days. Now, like my mother had been twenty years before, I was experiencing an American winter.

One evening I waited shivering outside New York's Lincoln Centre, watching my breath as it escaped and floated in the frigid air. For a while after leaving my mouth and nostrils, it hung there, straining to make icicles in mid-air, a puff of my essence which held its shape for only a little while before it ran into the oncoming Broadway crowds streaming around me. Everyone was muffled to the hilt to protect against the plummeting temperature of Manhattan on New Year's Eve. I was as frozen as the theatregoers shuffling past me – vertical rolls of coats, jacket, hats and scarves – trying to camouflage themselves from the purview of the Arctic weather as if it was a sniper who had come to pick them off one by one.

Many shows proclaimed themselves from the theatre billboards, but I was here to see one specific dance company.

'You're going to New York?' someone enquired when I told them about my plans to stop in the States en route to Saint

Vincent. 'You have to see Alvin Ailey. They are like nothing else on this planet!' they said.

When I read the history of the dance company and how their pieces and choreography were also rooted in gospel, the songs of slaves and the history of the Black struggle against oppression, I knew that I would have to judge for myself. That's why I found myself standing off Broadway in the freezing cold. Many other people were around me and waiting too.

That night was amazing because I did fall in love with the Alvin Ailey American Dance Theater company and specifically their suite of dances entitled *Revelations*, first performed in 1960, and its individual pieces, which I would come back to see time after time through the ensuing decades – 'Fix Me Jesus Fix Me', 'Wade in the Water', 'Rocka My Soul in the Bosom of Abraham'. I saw why the Alvin Ailey dance company drew people so faithfully to see them because of their ability to soulfully render the realities of life through movement and music: to show how dance could be dreamlike and visionary and yet still stay utterly faithful to the human experience. These dances weren't just about artistry and choreography; they were also about healing. And on that cold New Year's Eve night, as I travelled back to Saint Vincent for the first time in twenty years, I began to find healing too.

After New Year, we began the next stage of our journey to Saint Vincent. At that time there were no direct flights from the US or UK and so we first flew to and set up camp in Barbados for a few days. We spent the time swimming, sitting on beaches and drinking in bars, but as each day rolled by I became more and more tense. Mentally, as much as I could, I prepared to get moving and to sink myself into a hole where I thought I would have no memory of anything familiar, only feelings and reactions.

That wasn't true though: thoughts of heavy purple mangoes and golden apples, the pineapple I grew from a discarded crown and could call my own, stories of Arawaks and Caribs, black sand beaches and the Dry River raced through my mind. They emerged and bobbed about on the surface of my consciousness before submerging again, glistening in an unexplained light like an abandoned bodyboard that refused to come to shore.

I wondered what was playing with my memories while I slept, adding sound and colour, spraying weakly held recollections with texture and perhaps rewriting history to assuage past guilts. I did not know if the images I had held on to had any strong meaning and effect in my current life. They could have been just tarnished and expired currency, battered and faded from jostling with more vibrant and recent experiences – less than dreams, just dusty and inconvenient antiques. But I could not be sure.

It was going to be hard to be back – I had bad memories of being in Saint Vincent as a child, separated from my parents and thrust into uncaring hands. I was unsure what ghosts and demons were waiting for me, although the chief conductor of my pain had long since passed away. It was going to be a journey of fear and trepidation that also promised discovery.

I took out the black notebook which had travelled with me from Aotearoa, stuffed with letters from friends in the UK and NZ Department of Conservation leaflets, and started to write down everything I experienced, everything that I felt.

The time came to head to Grantley Adams Airport again and we dived through the crowds of people to an empty and cold check-in completely free of the gaggles of American tourists who had flooded through Arrivals with us a few days before. Our fellow passengers were locals. Their accessories were bags holding clothes and newspapers, baskets of groceries and cooked food, not sun lotion, dark glasses or beachwear.

As a child in Saint Vincent, I remembered visiting my mother's well-off brother and sitting on the floor of his small study reading about krakens and maelstroms that, even though I was safe on land, I felt were lying in wait to engulf me. Saint Vincent was the centre of my own personal vortex, trying to suck me back and downwards ever since I had been plucked away from the island as a child in the 1970s.

Only a couple of dozen people joined us at the gate. I wondered whether all these other people were being pulled westwards too, in the same way as me, as we all crammed onto the Carib Express flight to Arnos Vale. But in reality, our thoughts and motivations were as separate as the islands of an archipelago, even though we were bound together in the skin of that small aeroplane.

The plane groaned as it strained to get high enough to be able to complete the coming descent safely. There was barely enough time to drink a glass of red wine and decide which side of the plane would give the best view of our destination, because suddenly Saint Vincent thrust itself up out of the ocean: a verdant, unsubdued fortress appearing where before there had been nothing except bright blue sea. It was lush, fertile and mountainous, and huge and small at the same time. I had waited two decades to feel the thrill of that sight again. *My* island, to me the only treasure island in the world.

I did not remember the coast, the flat skirt of land and houses dancing at the feet of jagged mountains. But I could recall the dragon that as a child I thought lived under the high and undulating line of hills above the airport, stretching deep into the sea, sleeping, breathing, snuffling and waiting for someone to come back and believe in it again.

We walked along the tarmac towards the small, low customs building in the warm twilight air, invisible insects humming a chorus of welcome. To the left, hemmed in behind a line of barriers, there was a gaggle of greeters, any of whom could have been relatives of mine. And just as we were about to enter the doorway, I saw my favourite uncle, Cluston, casually chatting and joking with an immigration officer and himself slow to recognise his nephew. I had loved his jovial, devil-may-care manner ever since he drove me round the clifftops of the island in his car when I visited as a child with my dad and because of how fun he was when he came to stay with us in Luton, over for a training course for police officers from the Commonwealth.

The customs officer's gaze took in my girlfriend. 'How long are you staying?'

'Two weeks,' she replied, and he stamped her passport for a month's stay.

'Your father is a Vincentian?' he asked me, knowing already because my uncle had told him.

I nodded.

'You… you can stay here for as long as you like.'

'Hello, Monty!' And just like that, I was given back my island name by my beloved Uncle Cluston. It was strange and familiar at the exact same time, no longer a cumbersome family middle name or piss-taking tease. Even the Caribbean inflection was different and comforting, not the screeching, teasing 'MON-teeeeeeee' I had so often heard shrieked loudly through cackling playground taunts, but a deep bass greeting full of warmth and welcome.

Before leaving Aotearoa, I had talked with a group of local Māori Deaf people about names and the many by which we are known throughout our lives. First names, Christian names, middle names, surnames, nicknames. On that day, we explored names as labels that people give to us or that we attach to ourselves, like white workplace stickers scrawled on by chunky marker pens. Clinging to us like the tags on our luggage, verifying the baggage we take with us across borders.

I stood in front of the whiteboard in a room at the community centre and shared the names that had been given to me. I went over the name they had all seen written down – 'Alexis' – and then signed 'Smiler' – the arc of forefinger and thumb that formed the nickname local people had given me. I loved how in sign language the flow of fingers and arms could capture the essence and identity of someone: the curve of a grin, the unique curls of a woman's hair, how someone stood, or in my case, my height, colour and the beam that people seemed to think I always carried on my face (not true). For everyone in the room, sign was not a substitute or poor cousin of spoken language but instead its powerful and usually superior equivalent.

What I could also share with the group was my other name. I was given Alexis as my first name, but to my mum and dad, uncles and aunties, my brother, sister and cousins in Luton, and my relatives back in the West Indies – to my family – I was always Monty, my shortened middle name. Not barked in the brisk, military, upper-class style that my schoolmates affected so that they could take the piss, but pronounced by those close to me as a soft and loving *'Mun-tee'*. Monty, the name that my mum struggled to avoid using when she called up the stairs for me to come down and speak to my friends, who were listening on the phone she held out in her hand.

When the boys at school found out my middle name and teased me in the breaks between lessons, I cursed my parents' choice and felt embarrassed. But now I thought about how I abruptly stopped calling my mum and father Mummy and Daddy because of that same teasing, despite the fact that all the words we used for each other were signifiers of love and just the same as in most other West Indian families. We let go of so much because we are told we should feel ashamed to keep holding on.

I did not understand the significance of my *other* name until I got back to the Caribbean and uncovered the power of the sense of belonging that its intimacy gave to me. The name Monty bundled together all that I was and that I belonged to. Here a name was not just a name; it was a song of connection. For some reason, I remembered the family we lived next door to in Saint Vincent during our childhood stay: Gretchen, Gideon and Gareth. The rhythm of their names was a reminder of how poetry was spun through the speech of my people just like the repeating play of the names of my uncles Edson, Cluston, Alston and my father Winston. Here people would even call out, giving me an entirely different surname, *Rogers!* – my grandfather's. My father had travelled across the Atlantic proudly under his mother's name, but here, under the Caribbean sun, I came back to find out I was part of a far wider family clan.

There was a weird cacophony of animal noises in the morning in Saint Vincent. Dogs barking, donkeys braying and goats bleating as they meandered down the road, unseen birds tweeting and chittering while chickens clucked and cocks crowed. And on top of this, all the people chatting as they walked down the road which passed behind and above my parents' house, voices filtering in through the mosquito mesh of my bedroom window. A man in a blue Adidas tracksuit would walk down the road at dawn blasting out reggae from an invisible device so that it seemed as if the music was travelling with him like an unseen cloak.

It usually rained just after dawn, the winds bringing clouds which appeared out of nowhere even on mornings which had seemed clear and sunny. The sound of these deluges would cancel all other noises even without accompanying thunder and lightning.

One Sunday, I took my father to a service at the Anglican church on the hill overlooking the village, and a downpour arrived, its roar bursting in through the open doors and drowning out the priest's sermon. The floor shook under our feet, and it felt as if the whole church might come loose and slide into the sea. When I sat on my parents' porch in the morning, the rain would not pause, streams cascading from the gutters. I would sit with the torrent, its presence hiding me and yet also a curtain folding me into this village of villages. Eventually the sun would manage to push rays through the clouds, emerging to shine on me, although still the raindrops came down until finally, as the sunlight became brighter and warmer, the quiet came.

In the early morning, before it was too hot, I walked up to the cemetery to experience the wonder of gazing back on the village of Biabou. In the cemetery, and as the wind blew in from the sea, I made reacquaintance with my father's mother Esther and other relatives that had long ago passed.

On the way back down, I stopped and chatted with a local, Dante, who always wanted serious cash but who on this occasion had to be content with change and a Ju-C that I got him from Cassian's shop. Although I had come from England, I was not rich in the way that everyone seemed to think I was.

In the afternoon, I sought out another relative, Miss Vita, and we sat together exploring her gigantic Bible with more recent handwritten stories recorded in its back pages of births, deaths and multiple marriages. From her house, on a hill which stepped up to the mountains, Miss Vita showed me her view: coconut trees parading down the black sand, out of the reach of a baffled sea, unable to drag the whole world into its stormy grip. Together we shared the best sights of all, with a seat perfect for liming and catching up on whispers.

Everywhere I stopped to talk to someone I found a connection, but I soon figured out that these bonds linking me and my fellow Vincentians did not travel only in straight lines but sometimes took sideways leaps and bounds like the goats which scurried away as I passed them in the lanes around the village. At each stop – not just in Biabou, but also in Dickson where my mother was from and all across the island – I was introduced to potential and actual relatives.

'Ah who is yuh parents?'

'Wey dey from?'

'Yuh face favour yuh daddy so nah!'

'Woy! Yuh nah know yuh mus' call me cousin!/aunty!/ nephew!'

'So and so marry to so and so and dem have two pickney! An' him have t'ree outside!'

Many of the homes I was invited into were modest, with walls of wooden boards in the main and sometimes holding only one room. They perched on hillsides with drainage channels furrowed in the ground and yapping dogs outside which possessed more bark than bite. In the remote inland villages water was still fetched from standpipes in the road.

My Uncle Erdrin told me how he and my father had grown up in a small house like this with their six brothers and their mother, my grandmother Esther. His tales of how poor they were made my heart ache, but he also made me cry with laughter.

He told me how one day he was standing in the queue for water and the other village children had recoiled from him, pointing and shaking their heads. It took a while for him to realise that the cause of their simultaneous merriment and disgust was a crapo – a toad – poking its head out of the hole of the calabash he was using to collect the family's water. The toad's body was too big for it to fall out just by tipping the gourd, but his family were too poor to go without their 'boly', so he could not smash it. Instead, he and his brothers had to spend some time using sticks, prodding and poking to ease the reptile out. The very next day he was in the queue again, with the self-same calabash, suffering teasing by all the other children once more because my grandmother could not afford to replace it.

Despite their poverty, Erdrin, my father and other uncles had studied and worked hard to enable them to travel overseas. They ended up in Luton, Reading, High Wycombe or on the merchant ships, all the while sending home for their mother single five-pound and ten-pound notes tucked into separate envelopes which meant the world.

I revisited my maternal grandmother Henrietta's crumbling wooden house up in Dickson, the volcanic slopes of La Soufrière rising above. When we were little, my brother, sister and I had lived a short while with her before our stay on the island came to an end and our mother came to take us back to England. This was the house where, as a child, I had slept under my grandmother's bed after reading myself into tiredness by the light of an oil-wick lantern.

The drives to find these places on winding roads along clifftops and valley ridges were devotional processions through scenes of Eden-like beauty. In my journal, its pages still expanded by postcards and copies of letters sent from Aotearoa, I tried to carry on recording my wonderment:

Banana cathedrals, dusty, crumbling aisles and naves,
Strewn with fronds thrown in hosannas.
Arching spines holding up the weight of hallucinatory moun-
tains,
And green curtains blocking and sucking down light.
Blue bags line the way to Georgetown.
A river twice crossed,
Both ways a foaming pit passed where clothes
washers bend and pound.
All this to see Pam
A playmate of old, up in old Dickson
Who shared sleeps under grandma's bed,
In a house that could walk,

Or collapse onto its knees.
Past the provisions shop on the left, right by the guava tree,
Arrival and redemption;
The sun has seared my blackness into my skin.

Later, I watched twilight begin in the village to which my
mother and father had come back for their retirement, and I
thought simply that God had created the sweetest screensaver
in the peach clouds and the disappearing sun. At my feet, tiny
black ants clustered around the shell of a fallen gecko. All the
essential elements of life had been taken away and all that was
left was a husk of outer gecko, a whisper of skin and filaments
held in place by a filigree of bones.

During the night, I was woken again by the rain. It rained for
hours, water streaming through the ocean winds which buffeted
the house my parents had built. But still I slept and dreamt and
remembered the words of my father's friend Cassian at the central
shop, an echo of what I already knew: 'Yes, you're home now.'

Back in my parents' front room in England, I had looked so
many times at a single dot on a page in the middle of our worn
atlas. The few Carib, French and English place names – which
did not fit onto the tiny, green-contoured oval and overflowed
into the sea – were full of lilt and history, reflecting the tugs-
of-war between colonising European powers and indigenous
people. Now, on returning, I discovered that the name for the
fat, lazy cane toads came from the French '*crapaud*' and a '*petit*'
was still the way to ask for the tot of fierce rum that men gulped

in between slapping down domino pieces with enough force to rock and shudder the tables.

Everything seemed to grow madly on the island. Trees bearing golden apples, avocado, guava, sugar plums, orange and coconut tangled on the seductive slopes with verdant troops of banana trees. Twenty years before, I had taken away vivid recollections of giant land snails and gorgeous hummingbirds, praying mantises which I trapped in jars and would feed innocent flies to, and vicious Jack Spaniard hornets whose sting everyone feared. But now, even in daylight, insects seemed harder to find, and the noise of creatures in the night's darkness was a more muted buzz.

I thought that my child's imagination might have exaggerated all the things I thought I had seen before. But my relatives told me how in the decades between my visits, small farmers had drowned their hillside pockets of land in pesticide, wanting to ensure they had enough healthy produce to load onto the banana boat which sat waiting every week in Kingstown harbour.

I went up mountain too with my Uncle Fitzroy and tried to help, endeavouring to cut down the heavy bunches in the same way as him, without chopping myself or letting them plummet to the ground bruised. But regardless of my care, I watched with surprise as he detached any of the fat, green fruit that had even the slightest blemish, discolouration or imperfection. He knew they would be rejected by the graders at the boxing plant as unworthy and unsaleable for the tastes and baskets of shoppers browsing the aisles of supermarkets back in the UK.

I remembered how I had found a new voice on the island twenty years before. When I arrived in Saint Vincent as a little ten-year-old boy and went to school in my immaculate new uniform of khaki shorts and white, short-sleeved shirt, I astounded my new classmates with my deep, English tones. But back in England again a year later, I was transformed into the pupil who couldn't be understood by the other children who surrounded and jostled me in the primary school playground, mocking what they called my 'Rasta accent'. Soon I lost that voice – as a teenager I was not able to carry off a cool patois like kids who had never been to the places of their parents' birth like I had. But now, a change crept back into my voice after only a few days as I reflexively followed the flow of the spoken loops and cadence of the people I spent my days with.

From my parents' veranda, I watched the passers-by in the narrow road below, carrying their heavy loads of provisions to be transported from village to town and from town to village. Seeing how they managed their burden, it came back to me how at my Luton high school I had been teased, not only for my middle name but also the shape of my head. The other children called me 'Beanhead'. But now coming back to Saint Vincent, I saw and knew that my head was beautiful and exactly as it should be for all the places my ancestors had come from.

As the end of our time in Saint Vincent neared, we returned to the north of the island, and with my quiet and serious Uncle Fitzroy and an exuberant youth nicknamed Handyman as guides, we climbed the volcano starting in hot, thick, dense rainforest where the fallen leaves were as big as rafts.

Handyman was a young, handsome man, strong and agile, and he would die years later in a cutlass fight caused by a dispute over drugs. The heights and deep valleys hid much from the gaze of the police, including the fields of weed cultivated mainly by Rastas and other peaceful growers like Handyman. But the mountains could not shield these small farmers or the island from the seep of organised crime and smuggling, and their associated violence.

By the time we reached the summit, our heads were in the clouds, surrounded by mists that hid the sea and island below. The fog stopped us seeing across to the other side of the magnificent crater which was terraced around its inner curve. In the middle, a huge plug of rock still smoked, the former lake and courageous rowers long ago evaporated into legend. The volcano had been dormant since 1979, but still I grinned at the story of how my cousin Jane had run a crazy, screaming sprint down the road yards ahead of her astonished fellow villagers, because someone had whispered rumour to her of eruption to come.

The fourteenth of March was a national holiday to commemorate the life and death of the island's national hero, Paramount Chief Joseph Chatoyer, who was killed by the British at Dorsetshire Hill in 1795 during the second Carib War. Chatoyer was Garinagu – born of the proud and fiercely resistant warriors who arose from the mixing of the indigenous Carib tribes, who populated the island before the British arrived, and the escaped and shipwrecked African slaves who had arrived amongst them.

Across the island, people packed picnics, dressed up and crowded into the buzzing minibuses – which terrifyingly careered around the curving, potholed country roads – to set off for trips out in the sunshine. They were celebrating their nation's freedom and self-determination. We did the same with a group of family and friends I had rediscovered in Biabou, people who welcomed and remembered me from my long-ago time on the island as a child. They only had good memories of the time I had spent with them.

Our eager plan was to travel over on the ferry, which daily tracked southwards down the islands between Saint Vincent and Grenada, to explore the new airport on Bequia, the nearest and largest of the Grenadines. Of all the days I spent on the island, this was the most beautiful, and after we returned, I sat on the balcony and wrote in simple verse about the things we had seen and done:

Biabou on a clear wet morning
Greets Monty and K, Monty still yawning.
Judy and Fitzroy, amaze that we up
For our journey to Kingstown in the back of a truck.
'Alyuh mek de boat late!' moan the people for Mustique.
'When we gwan get on?' the Bequia crowd bleat.
We mek tru de channel and Judy not sick,
Tho' de waves mek

She pull face,
Like she swallow lipstick.
We lan' 'pon de wharf and head up de hill,
Ann ah cuss everybody – de water too still.
Hulk and Anthony try to chat up all de gal
And we pass by a blockout, all dancing and smiles.
We check 'pon de airport; we have to take photo
'Fore spending the afternoon 'pon
Strong rum and pejo.
Cards slap on de table and rattle de glass.
We come 'pon a Rasta who try overcharge
Till we tell him we know price inna this yard.
We nah get de mango but we have a good laugh.
It time to reverse now and gwan home sleepy and proud,
And dis time de porpoises come roun' and sing by de bow.

On my last evening there was a power cut, and I needed my Uncle Edson to come round and unlock the cupboard which held the candles. They were labelled 'Olympian premium non-drip' and I wondered if that meant they could light my way forever.

I could not see the sea now, but I heard the hum of the wind – rising, picking up and fading away, carrying with it the sounds of a distant party.

We talked about house pipes and cruise ships and travelling, and then he was gone, leaving me to get ready to fly back to London. Mentally I was already in the part of my journey when the plane is circling the port of entry, the 'fasten seat belt' signs on and the in-flight movie finished. My descent had begun, ears popping and air crackling as last-minute touches, events and preparations rushed by.

I already knew that an opportunity to return to the Southern Hemisphere was waiting for me. I did not know when I would come this way again. Part of me was scared at the thought of what I might lose, the end of the rarity of being and feeling special. I worried that my travels would make me just another peddler with a pile of photographs and a bag of undeveloped rolls of film. But now I felt happy and proud to be an itinerant from England with Aotearoa in my heart and Saint Vincent in my bones. I was on the way back to the other places that were home to me, knowing now that I could have more than one.

I turned on National Radio one last time, and as I sat in the kitchen, the exhortations of the Banana Rally up at New Grounds where my mother had taught many years ago bounced round my parents' house: 'Forward ever, backward never!'

Catherine

May 1812, The Atlantic

When the ship Catherine had clambered onto the night before sailed out of Kingstown harbour, the air was still filled with haze and ash. The eyes and noses of the inhabitants who had to stay on the island streamed constantly from the volcanic fumes. La Soufrière had finally erupted in April 1812 after weeks of tremors and rumbles, and the British plantation and colonial officials, and the few French farmers, were of course the first to flee, either to the safety of Barbados 100 miles to the east, or back to Europe.

A few years later, J.M.W. Turner would produce a dramatic portrait of the mountain, satanic and brooding as its summit exploded. But he did this from the safe English shores of Kent. His artistic interpretation was based on a sketch hastily captured by a British planter called Keane as he fled, leaving behind the people he owned as slaves and his estates.

Other than that painting, which Turner displayed at the Royal Academy exhibition of 1815, what stayed in the memories of those who escaped the island was the pall of smoke which hung above the island like the fist of God. Although their noses would eventually be clear of the stench of sulphur, the image of that cloud stuck in their minds even when they reclaimed their trappings of privilege in places where nature was more subdued.

The landowners had already thought themselves persecuted and disadvantaged by the abolition of the transatlantic trade in enslaved people in 1807 (although the practice of slavery itself in British colonies was not abolished until 1834). On reaching England after the eruption of La Soufrière, they thought themselves ruined and asked His Majesty's Government for financial support to deal with the losses they had incurred. Their petition stated that parts of the island 'have suffered in an extreme degree; the showers of volcanic matter ... having covered the whole surface of the ground [in that area] about ten inches deep ... but most providentially, not many lives were lost'.

'Not many lives were lost,' they said, perhaps no more than three dozen Blacks. Catherine heard her new master and mistress discuss the parliamentary debates nearly a year after the eruption, and if she closed her eyes, she could imagine those whose lungs choked in the acrid smog or the weak and frail who could not outrun the flows of hot mud that had raced down the dry river gullies. She thought about those whose livelihoods must have disappeared as the sun's disappearance caused bananas, cane and all other fruit and crops to shrivel and perish. She imagined the hellish peril of the Caribs whose enclave on the northern tip of the island was cut off from any possibility of a southward route to safety – they had no escape unless into the sea.

The plantation owners went back to their country estates in England and made investments elsewhere while they waited for the land to be ready for the labourers to work again. They took with them back to England a few of those who had been enslaved upon their plantations to make the voyage comfortable and to enhance their status when they returned to polite society.

After working her way up from the cane fields to the plantation house to help the mistress, Catherine had gained enough experience to gain ship's passage as a chambermaid. Each long day she had to complete her duties of cleaning cabins, fetching food and emptying pails of slop and human waste into the sea. But her mother had taught her to sew well, and the white ladies on the boat took quite a fancy to her work. They gave her cotton, which after her other work, sitting cross-legged on the deck and squinting in the dim lantern light, she crocheted in the evenings to make fine embroidery for them. Then, with the other female slaves, she would collapse onto the rough-hewn boards in the bowels of the ship where their sparse coverings could never dry out from the sea damp which slid down the boards of the hull.

On most nights Catherine cried, trying to stifle her sobs into her hands so as not to disturb the sleeping bodies hemmed against her. Oblivion came just a couple of hours before the bell sounded for the morning watch, only for her to be haunted by dreams of the loss of weight and warmth when the cold hands of the overseer took her son from her. The other dreams she had were of how she would punish the man who took her child to be exhibited in Kingstown.

As Catherine's eyelids trembled, a disintegrating playbill soaked by her tears stayed clenched in her hand. Catherine could not read, but one of the other slaves had passed it to her after finding it in a mouldering pile of newspapers. They had been brought out from London for the plantation owners, but after the ship's rapid turnaround they now lay discarded in a corner.

An advertisement on the sheet proclaimed the delights of 'John Richardson's Portable Theatre'. The performances were to be held at a Michaelmas Fair in 1811 at the Market Square, Marlow. On successive nights, the main act had been a play – either The Turkish Slave, Monk and Murderer *or* The Skeleton Sceptre. *But in the bottom corner, a drawing illustrated the speciality act which followed each performance. A small boy dressed as Cupid with a quiver of arrows slung across his back and a golden earring in one ear, the snake he was clasping almost distracting the reader from the patchwork of black and white across his skin. The Beautiful Spotted Boy.*

Part III

TARANAKI

Mountain Life

I sat in the winter sunshine, a light breeze brushing my face as I thought about what being in Aotearoa was doing to me. I was scribbling notes directly onto the pages of my book – a weather-beaten second-hand copy of *Social Work Radical Essays* printed in Queensland. I had picked it up for five dollars on a trawl of a dense, narrow-aisled Whangārei bookshop months before when I had been an entirely different person.

I wrote another line in the margins: 'Can I have fun in New Plymouth?' and 'What has changed me?' Alongside the gutter I had simply let words fall in a vertically descending line: 'I'm… falling… asleep'. I did not feel that I was defacing the book – the pages were already threatening to come away from the spine of the cover – but I was in a reflective mood that afternoon.

The chapter I was reading was entitled 'Professionalism'. Another chapter, and perhaps the one which had caught my eye as I had flicked through it in the Northland bookstore, had as its title the non-ironic quote: 'The Blacks in South Brisbane Are Just a Mob of Metho-Drinking No-hopers'. I reflected that perhaps it was easier to relax and breathe in my skin here than in the country on the other side of the Tasman Sea.

Days before I had heaved the green-and-purple rucksack that had travelled with me around the world into the boot of my small blue Holden and headed down State Highway 3 to New Plymouth, a place I had barely heard of. Halfway into that four-hour journey, the colours of the leaves on the trees told me that I was arriving somewhere very different from Northland. Further south on the North Island, it was a surprise and delight to find that four seasons marked the passage of the year again. During the drive, there was a stretch where the hues of the trees on either side of the road blinded my eyes with autumnal glory, a blazing ribbon of red, gold and yellow threading through volcanic hills and across grassy plains.

Like Saint Vincent, Taranaki was dominated by the gaze of a mountain, and Te Maunga Taranaki looked how my childhood imagination always thought a mountain should look. It rose above expanses of dairy pastures, ruling its landscape without competition on the horizon except often a crown of cloud and mist. Its glorious, snow-capped peak could puncture the mundanity of a boring workday, relieve the load of any chores or bills to pay and make my initial loneliness feel well worth the sight of this natural wonder.

Like La Soufrière in Saint Vincent, Mount Taranaki was a volcano, but unlike its Caribbean counterpart, it had not had a major eruption for more than 140 years. Back in Saint Vincent, I had heard La Soufrière's eruptions counted down through family generations.

In 1979, my aunties hid inside while the air grew acrid and poisonous, and falling stones were flung several miles and rained down halfway across the island. My grandparents lived through the evacuations and terrors of 1902 when the sky turned black in the daytime. Beyond that, in 1812 and 1718, columns of ash and smoke punched angry holes into the Caribbean sky as La Soufrière's colossal belches split the earth's skin. In the decades between eruptions, forebears whose names I did not know had been able to march the trails upwards between gigantic boulders vomited out from beneath the crust and across gullies gouged out by lava flows. Perhaps they ventured out in Church groups on Sunday outings or joined up in gangs of free-spirited young men and women, swinging cutlasses to cut through the native bush and using their free hands to hoist baskets of food and drink.

Both volcanoes were frequently enveloped in mist and were shrouded even more deeply in the invisible clouds of human history. La Soufrière was a green colossus, still steaming and heaving, shuddering the mantle beneath, shaking its foundations and trying to wrench the island free of its socket in the earth's crust. In winter, Taranaki was flanked with snow and bided its time as it surveyed the North Island landscape that Māori legend said the mountain god had walked across in grief at the loss of his beloved. I wondered if one day the mountains might talk to each other or whether they already extended subterranean filaments of lava which met deep inside the earth, geological pulses answering each other's beat.

It was winter in July, with clear blue skies and only wisps of cloud to convince us that we could not get sucked off the face of the planet. The sun and snow-covered mountain were behind me. New Plymouth life played itself out under Taranaki's regal stare and in the path of the ash plume from Ruapehu, a smoke ring frozen in time on a not-so-distant horizon. Two seagulls played tag above me, cartwheeling in the part of the sky that was still blue, while in the other corner, over the port and my rented cottage, a cloud functioned as a shutter, blinking the sun in and out.

Whoever was behind the camera would capture images of me on the café terrace where an art exhibition was being held inside. Above me, I could hear teacups clinking in the room which held the paintings and which had expansive views of the Tasman and the rain which was heading inland. A thin, brown railway line burrowed along the coast interminably, like a headless parasite which had lost attachment to its host, blindly slithering its way to an exclamatory aperture miles away.

I could smell people as they passed – *Coffee, gin and Old Spice must weld to skin*, I thought – and I wondered what scents would define me and whether people had been able to sense my difference in the Caribbean.

A dress some might have called call too thin for a Taranaki winter rustled in the wind. With the local wisdom I had acquired in just a few weeks, I wondered if the breeze was from the sea or the mountain. It was important in Taranaki, because for sure there was a difference in the kind of ice it drove into your bones. I found exploring the land to be as raw and refreshing as the stabbing cold that accompanied the slabs of polar air which migrated northwards occasionally, moving ponderously up from Antarctica to nestle over Aotearoa's islands.

A national park encircled the mountain, and around that was the wider girdle of fertile and flatter Taranaki lands which pressed out into the Tasman Sea from the west coast of the North Island. This countryside felt peaceful and in no way tumultuous to an outsider like me. But I explored the region's history too – *Ask That Mountain: The Story of Parihaka* was a treasured gift from a friend – and in my reading discovered that in the 1860s and onwards it had been the theatre of continuing battles between the British and Māori tribes in brutal conflicts where rape, the murder and kidnapping of children, decapitation, enslavement and exile were used as tools of warfare. Māori fought to hold onto their lands, the British to occupy and grab those lands for settlers.

In 1865, the New Zealand Government confiscated the mountain itself from Māori in the pursuit of quelling resistance. For Māori, it was the British, not all *pakeha* (Europeans), who were the focus of their attacks and resistance; in the journals and notes of colonial soldiers, the rebellious Māori were dehumanised – just like the Garinagu on Saint Vincent seventy years before – as 'niggers' and 'black vermin'.

For neither the Garinagu or Māori was land a commodity to be traded or given away – it held the essence of existence and identity. Māori, as indigenous people, claimed land not in the sense of possession but as the natural consequence of being part of it – part of each other – and to naturally care for it and to be its guardians. Soil, water and land were *taonga* (treasures). '*I am the land; the land is me. One cannot not survive without the other.*'

The sun winked once more then scuttled away: kittenishly, I thought – a dignified old queen gathering her robes at the end of the day. Today had been warm and life-filling, even though the air on my skin told me this was not how I was used to July feeling. It felt like I had been reset – perhaps my internal programmes had been altered in the Caribbean. Default settings were subtly changed, and fundamental assumptions had been taken away.

As I got up, readying myself to leave, I felt compelled to make sure everyone knew that I was taking back my plate, cup and saucer to the counter. I think I was the only one to do this. But then it was clear that I was not from these parts, and how I looked and my words and manner would always spell that out. I thought it was a self-awareness that Black people feel wherever our skin marks out our difference, a preparation for being focused on and readiness for being singled out for blame.

I remembered the burning humiliation I had felt when, returning to Whangārei, a coach driver had tapped me on the head when his bag fell from his seat as if I had done it through the powers of telekinesis from a row away. I felt shame at being patted on the head like a child, anger that I did not react more angrily to it and, weirdest of all, a surreptitious feeling of guilt that perhaps I had been responsible for this quirk of gravity after all.

Despite these cultural dissonances, I thought that I was settling easily and happily into life in New Plymouth. The town's publicity, with sincerity and happy effectiveness, proclaimed 'COME TO LIFE' and 'S'miles better'. To me it was a place of kindness and friendship, and it felt like I had found another place that I could call home. I was surrounded by a close and loving group of New Plymouth friends who welcomed me into their city and their lives.

Before I left Auckland, I took time to go out to the movies. I rarely went to the pictures, but when I did it always felt like a really special occasion. On a screen in Whangārei, Antonio Banderas swaggered through the Mexican desert in *Desperado*, igniting pyrotechnics in the same way that my connection with my friends Rose and Natalee had lit up my time in Northland. Seeing London and Black British faces in Michael Leigh's *Secrets and Lies* in Auckland was an urgent reminder of England when I was at my most homesick, even though as I was coming out of the cinema, what I saw was the Rangitoto volcano rising out of the sea across Mission Bay not East London tower blocks.

The film my friends and I went to see that night, *Broken Arrow*, starred John Travolta and Christian Slater in a nineties 'high concept' movie involving an officer in the US Nuclear Protection Force gone rogue. I loved it. Afterwards we all sat in McDonald's, munched on our burgers, and deconstructed how much of a badass John Travolta was, and how we secretly liked him much more than the saintly Slater.

I looked behind me and saw a picture of a vintage, dark-green car on the wall. It was one of those items of fake memorabilia that pubs and fast-food outlets used to give an impression of their heritage and authenticity. The image was filled with happy white people whose clothes and hats proclaimed the 1950s, but ahead of the journey I was due to make the following day it was the caption running across the top of the image which caught my eye: *'New Plymouth. Packed with value and ready to prove it!'*

Now I was ready to head home. I walked towards the headland around the corner from my cottage in Moturoa where in 1868 a British force of 200 soldiers lost a quarter of their number in battle against Māori warriors. I watched the sun set on the Sugar Loaf islands while paragliders soared above the beach but level with me, as if they might come in to land on my cliff.

A grass-lined path took me down to the beach whose dark colours had been created by Taranaki Maunga exactly as La Soufrière had done through the aeons in Saint Vincent. Black sand had bounded my life, and now I let it run through my hands again. I picked up a single pale and smooth grey pebble banded with striations of geological murmurs carried down through the ages like light across the universe. I wondered at the pressures which had produced its beauty.

Placing it against my cheek, I felt the coldness of aeons and was calmed. I put it in my pocket and thought that perhaps everything was going to be alright. That if I allowed them, New Plymouth and the mountain would prove that to me.

Talk Radio

'He should be swinging in trees in the Congo.'

I stood stock-still, frozen with shock, in my cottage perched on the edge of the Tasman Sea. Anger and shame burnt through me because of what I had just heard on the radio that Sunday morning in 1996. Two years before, a Kenyan musician had been convicted and imprisoned in Aotearoa for having unprotected sex with several women knowing he was HIV positive but deliberately concealing that fact. The radio presenter I was listening to was bemoaning the cost to the taxpayer of keeping him in jail. I did not disagree with the sentence and had no opinion on where the offender should be incarcerated, but the racism of the words spoken that morning cut straight through me.

Aside from the vicious buzz of the host's voice in my head, the feeling that struck me most deeply was that of being alone. I knew that none of my family or friends had heard those words because they were 11,000 miles away in the UK. I did not have to do anything. I could let it go and try to continue quietly being a Black British man abroad and under the radar. I knew that staying quiet would be unnoticed and understandable, and I had an overwhelming realisation that there was no one else to help me with this. I knew all this was true, but I also knew that this was not a way I could allow myself to live and so, feeling sick with nerves, I picked up the telephone.

When I picked up the receiver and explained what I wanted to say to the show's researcher, I had a tremor in my voice and a feeling that inevitably the slick, bombastic presenter would make me sound tongue-tied and stupid or naive. Before speaking, I counted on my fingers the number of points I wanted to try to make, even if he cut me off.

I cannot remember exactly what I said. My words were lost in a blur of nervousness and anxiety. I know that I tried to get across to him and the invisible listeners the hurt and pain caused by his words: what it did to me and what it would do to all the people who shared my origins to have our dignity and humanity tossed away by being compared to animals. I don't think I was very eloquent, and I do not know if he listened to me. Later, a few weeks after this on-air confrontation, a harsh-voiced mechanic who I was speaking to on the phone about something else entirely took great pleasure in telling me that in his view I had indeed sounded like a dick. But regardless, somehow I got the words I wanted to say out and onto the airwaves.

After that Sunday morning, I complained about the presenter's racism to the New Zealand Broadcasting Standards Authority, and months later, my complaint was upheld. As part of that process I received a tape recording of the show, but it took twenty-two years, long after I was back in England, before I could bring myself to even think of listening to it, precisely because I was so anxious about how I had come across.

When I finally brought myself to play the recording, I found that I had been hiding from that exposure unnecessarily because it cut off before it reached the segment where I rang in – instead, it focused on the original provocative comments and the callers before me, who bemoaned the arrival of people who didn't have 'good Kiwi names' and needed language lessons on arrival in the country. They also seemed keen to attack the promotion of Māori language and culture which had so inspired and enthused me.

As I continued to work and make friends in New Plymouth, the callers and views on that show receded into the background of my memories of Aotearoa, whose overwhelmingly diverse and liberal people I loved and whose landscapes enraptured me. Listening and talking to that talk-show host was one of only two times when I felt that someone wanted to impose on me their assumptions and associations about where I or people of my skin colour came from. The other was a few weeks later when I went food shopping in Pak'nSave, and an old lady stopped me in the aisle, using her slight frame to block the passage of my trolley.

'And where are you from?' she enquired peering up at me.

I paused, wondering how to answer. I knew that she wanted me to name somewhere tropical that she could match with the darkness of my skin. It was an often-received enquiry which always had the potential to goad me into pricking the bubble of the questioner's stereotypes. I thought a while and then went for accuracy. 'I was born in London.'

'Ahh, how wonderful,' she said, hearing but not listening to me. 'You speak English even better than the rest of us.'

I laughed out loud, and, smiling widely and comfortably, moved on.

Dance, Dance, Dance

Part 1

I was more settled when I returned to the Southern Hemisphere after my time in the Caribbean, and being in New Plymouth felt right and familiar. In Whangārei, I had been growing used to the waves and currents of Aotearoa; in Taranaki I felt that I could swim. I could pick up the provincial paper, read the local news, politics and sports and feel instantly immersed and connected to what was going on. I had a group of friends, most of whom I met initially through my role with the Deaf Association, with whom I formed warm and enduring bonds. We played touch rugby together and built friendships through walks, midwinter festivals and nights out.

This city on the coast was washed over with waters of love and togetherness, and communality overflowed into the ocean. It did not take long for me to feel that New Plymouth was where I was from too and where I could always return to. At times, a made-up refrain would repeat in my mind: *England is my bed, Saint Vincent is my cradle and Aotearoa is my pillow.*

Six or seven of us went on a tramp to a remote hut near a small township which had styled itself the Republic of Whangamōmona, and we hiked through the bush and along paths partnered in bends and loops with the river which

marched below. As we walked, we spoke about what the maps
of our individual lives might look like. We imagined our own
pilgrimages, the track behind dotted with vain follies crowning
hilltops, marshy sloughs of despond bordered by imposing cliffs
of self-doubt. But for us all the horizon ahead was lit by new
sunshine, and by the side of the path were fields of swaying
cornflowers.

I took another journey with my friend Paula and her daughter,
a road trip along the meandering banks of the wide, muddy
Whanganui River. We headed for the small Māori township of
Hiruhama and the settlement of Parihaka where the poet James
K. Baxter had established the commune of Jerusalem. We spent
the journey singing and sharing our skills in taking naps, blowing
gum and stopping to play Poohsticks at isolated streams as we
went deeper into the 'wop-wops'. It was a still, sunny afternoon
when we reached Hiruhama and I felt a tingle across my whole
body when we found Baxter's grave and I realised that his middle
name and my surname were the same, and that perhaps I had
always been meant to travel there.

When the time came for me to leave New Plymouth and
Aotearoa, I held another leaving party. Friends I had made
gathered to farewell me and filled the living room of my little
cottage in Oceanview Parade, the windows open to the sounds
of the sea which threaded through the trees bordering the quiet
road in front of the beach.

The music for the party came from a small collection of
albums and tapes I had accumulated, piled up beside my cassette

recorder, and the one that got the most playtime was a compilation CD of reggae, RnB and soul I had picked up in Auckland. One track was by The Steppers whose chorus we waited for with tense anticipation so that we could roar together: 'WHO THE F**K IS ALICE?' Also in the stack was a twenty-track disc of rare, groove classics – *Dance Dance Dance*! – a triple exhortation to move our feet and bodies from artists like Grace Jones, The Isley Brothers, The O'Jays and Billy Preston. Orders we all obeyed, stomping and swaying while laughing ourselves silly at memories of the nine months we had shared together. And as the night grew late and the chat quieter, although no less engaged and warm, the background music was Jimmy Holiday crooning, 'Everybody needs help, help… sometimes…'

Even before the party, I had already begun clearing the cottage of much that I had gathered or that had become dear to me in Aotearoa. This time I knew that I was leaving to look for a permanent job back in the UK and that it would be a while before I came back to these islands. All the big items I did not want to struggle with on the long-haul flight had already left in the barrel which had been collected for shipping that week. In there were my hockey stick and squash racket, borrowed and given to me in Whangārei, and both of which had enabled so many social contacts through sport. I had also put in the barrel, well wrapped and protected, an abstract painting, *The Three Kings*, created by Paula, whose purple hues brought beauty and mystery to the walls of the little cottage by the sea and the sense that this home was all mine.

I kept my tapes and CDs with me though, for the party, and to listen to as I finished packing. In the stack was an album I had brought back to Aotearoa from my brief visit to New York and which had been with me my whole time in New Plymouth. The soundtrack of the Alvin Ailey American Dance Theater Company's performance of *Revelations* had kept me company on quiet Sundays and was the last plastic case to go into my luggage. For my Walkman during the journey, I kept a cassette of world music given to me by an English friend who had settled in New Plymouth; it had previously sustained me on a week-long jaunt over to Sydney and back. That friend's leaving gift to me was already on its way to London in the barrel: a framed drawing of Mount Taranaki, snow on its summit, a path leading to trees, pastures and farm buildings flanking its foothills.

I was leaving Taranaki and my cottage by the Tasman for city life in the UK, but coming with me was the music I had listened to as I found togetherness with people I could enjoy life with, no matter our differences of background.

Part 2

It was not until 2005 that I saw the Ailey company again. They came to what seemed to be their London home, Sadler's Wells Theatre in Islington.

My first ever trip to Sadler's had been a gift for my then partner so that she could see Matthew Bourne's *The Nutcracker*. From our seats in the upper circle, I leant over the railing, trying to float my head like a balloon into the vast space of the auditorium beneath me and ahead. I watched the smartly dressed audience arriving below, sliding into the aisles across withdrawn legs and nearly spilt drinks, holding their children, most of whom seemed to be little girls, by one hand and leading them without looking back, keen to sit down before the bell sounded and the lights went down. By the end, it was me who had been gripped by the show like those small children and who spent the performance perched on the edge of my seat.

When I was a teenager there was a time when spaces like Sadler's Wells would have felt alien and perhaps not meant for a boy from a working-class family like me. But as my interest grew beyond the weekly arthouse films I could see at the Library Theatre in Luton, I started escaping my hometown to find new worlds in the arts and exhibitions of the capital.

'Whatcha going there for?' a friend I met on the Leagrave station platform once asked me when I told him I was heading to London; I said I was going simply to browse and explore anything free, no set destination in my mind. I could not really explain it very well to him because the reasons were based on feelings and experiences that I found difficult to put into words.

I was drawn by exhibitions and installations, free music in the foyer of the Royal Festival Hall and then getting lost in the tight aisles of the Poetry Library on what seemed a hidden, semi-secret floor upstairs. My friend Dino and I discovered the Impressionist delights of the Courtauld Collection in a musty basement of University College London. The two of us exclaimed our wonder on seeing in the flesh, as it were, famous paintings whose abstract and pastel beauty I too would want to possess like the billionaires in newspaper headlines if I had their wealth.

But dance had not attracted me until I bought those Matthew Bourne tickets as a Christmas present. My partner was impressed, but it was me who, although quiet on the number thirty-eight bus back to Hackney, couldn't free my mind of the pirouettes and leaps, the pop art imagery and costumery.

And then I discovered the Ailey company. This performance in 2005 ended with the same piece that had warmed me in that freezing New York winter nearly a decade before: 'Rocka My Soul in the Bosom of Abraham'. Women paraded the stage in their finery, twirling their parasols, whilst the men strutted and preened like dandy cocks amongst the twirling, bright-yellow dresses. Their standing leaps looked effortless, though there was plenty of exertion on display as their bodies moved to reflect ours: the strength and muscularity of a woman lifting an undisclosed heavy object; runaway men panting, gasping and falling into a conjoined heap; impossibly long arms creating tubular, petal-like forms that spasmodically collapsed. It was this exuberant hymn to salvation that left me energised and bursting with happiness. Of course, the company received their usual standing ovation, the audience adoring their languidly elaborate on-stage choreography, a poetry which we could all feel described something of our own lives.

A few days later, I visited my sister at her workplace in the City of London. Her employers were sponsoring the Ailey UK tour that year, and a meeting room at my sister's office was packed, with standing room only, as office workers left their screens and keyboards to see the dancers who had exited rehearsals at Sadler's Wells for this promotional exercise. There was no pretence or artifice in the room though. Two members of the company sat behind a desk – tall, relaxed, elegant figures who held the complete attention of the room of upright professionals. They addressed those listening with a passion and eloquence that surprised me because of my own assumptions and naivety. After all, why shouldn't dancers use voice and words with the same skill as they used their bodies?

Any colours in the beige room came from the shirts and blouses of the office workers; the dancers themselves wore simple black and white. They spoke clearly but softly as they shared the history of the company. They described how Alvin Ailey had started it with a small group of Black dancers in 1958, and that it remained dedicated to preserving the uniqueness of the African American cultural experience but that for many years, as I had seen for myself, the dancers had come from varied ethnic and cultural backgrounds. Their words added to the feeling I already had that the Alvin Ailey American Dance Theater was a kind of artistic eighth wonder of the world because of its celebration of the African American cultural experience, which began with the songs of slaves in sun-drenched cotton fields, their servitude the legally prescribed foundation stone of a nation.

The dancers speaking in front of me were the embodiment of the excellence of the company's performers, drawing from the Black American wellspring of heritage, pain and growth. Through their bodies and movement, they shared those stories with the entire world. They were so clear and proud in their Blackness and carried their confidence in a way I had not often seen or felt myself; they were not cowed or wary in this room of finance professionals and had no need to prove their own expertise. In that glass and concrete building at the corporate heart of the City, they were like goddesses and gods come down to visit and to share out their blessings. They did not request their right to be there – they asserted and assumed it.

I wondered if I could be this way too, although I could not dream of moving like they did under the gaze of audiences of thousands. Could I perhaps shout or speak more powerfully or express myself clearly in some other way that made people pay attention to me? I listened to the dancers and began to think about and accept my own possibilities.

Part 3

The little girl in her sparkly, puffed skirt pirouetted amidst the crowds of people queuing for the interval bar at Sadler's Wells, her eyes wide with excitement. In her reverie and concentration, she created her own personal whirlpool, and the welldressed ticket holders for Alvin Ailey in 2017 – white people in more formal smart jackets and dresses, and many Black people in more vivid blacks, greens and yellows – flowed around her. Her movements were a lacuna in the bustle of humanity, with her red and pink tutu the swirling eye at the heart of the storm. Her mother stretched out a hand to gently pull her out of the way, not harshly but simply to bring her to nestle under the wing of a maternal arm, the girl's bigger brother tucked in on the woman's other side.

'Great, isn't it,' said the little girl's mother, looking up in the direction of where I hung around, companionless now and drink in hand. 'Is this your first time?'

'Yes. It's brilliant,' I said. 'And no, I have seen them many, many times now. I try to see them every time they come back to the UK.'

I turned to the little girl – her brother's eyes and attention were everywhere else in a room so ripe with distractions. 'Are you enjoying it?' I asked her.

'Yes!' she said, grinning. 'I love the dancers. I want to have a job like them when I'm big.'

Each time I had seen them since the first, the company had brought new work, new concoctions of verve, expression and physicality to challenge and beguile me. And I knew their artistry would always return fresh to me. Rebirth, transgression, redemption: the dancers journeyed through the baptismal waters, confessed their sins and expressed their joy to the audience. With their soulful account of the African American identity, they showed how dance could be beautiful, dreamlike, vision-ary – and still authentic and true. I never thought I 'could have a job like them' as that little girl aspired to, but I wanted to try to describe the emotions of watching to others so that they could experience it as well.

A year or so after the Alvin Ailey performance at Sadler's Wells, I found myself in the audience at the Lyric Hammersmith at a LIFT festival performance, sat with pencil and notebook in hand trying to balance both with a glass of wine. I had been asked to write a review of the show *Fatherland*.

When the lights went down, the stage filled with battalions, phalanxes of men moving, marching, grooving and growing. Men like the men I knew in my life. Imperfect, angry, vulnerable and sometimes beautiful. Young, middle aged and ageing in the margins. Men were given or took control of centre stage in the world outside the theatre, but it still felt revelatory to see how the floodlights shone on them – and on fatherhood – in this performance.

The coats stood out: the armour of manhood in the twenty-first century. Men in black, beige and tan coats; leather jackets; tracksuit tops and parkas. Faceless firemen in what might as well be hazmat suits in a nightmare of *X-Files* proportions. Men marching, swaying, writhing, climbing and dropping from the sky. Men using ladders and doorways to fly. Men gathered in a workers' or maybe hobos' circle around the glow of a bonfire and marching through the streets like a massed football army, but with flags that appeared to be made of delicate silk. The sole flash of colour was the red of a Man U top standing out for its brightness in the gloom as much as for its ancient sponsor's logo.

And only men's voices were heard – from baleful to operatic. At one stage, the thirteen men on stage were joined by massed voices from the aisles and circle. The men on stage, like the audience thankfully, were diverse in their ethnicities and accents. In myriad stunning ways, *Fatherland* expressed the profound verbatim testimony collected from provincial England and echoed through songs and chants against a pensive soundtrack that boomed and whispered. It told stories of harrowing sadness about fathers lost or never known. These were the stories of 'real' men – where 'real' means from Kidderminster, Stockport and Bewdley – and men who were emphatically still living that reality. Men who had not left to join the metropolitan elites.

The men in *Fatherland* did not want to leave their hometowns: one character was sure that the place you grew up in makes you who you are. And even if, like me, they had moved geographically, their hometown had not left them, in the same way that I was indelibly stamped with Made in Luton . This performance did not sneer at the vibrancy of small-town life or make up stereotypes about its grittiness and perceived mundanity. As much as anything else, *Fatherland* was a hymn to the small places. Biabou, Luton, Whangārei and New Plymouth waited in its wings.

The show was not just about fathers – it was very much about being a son too and the pain of one not being able to connect with the other. In the media, to be a contemporary father was almost automatically flawed – the relationship notable usually for both being needed and for being absent – and the paternal relationships of the men in *Fatherland* portrayed all those complexities and then some.

But *Fatherland* was not just a journey through the bad bits of being a man – it found ways to lift me into admiration and eventually joy. I smiled a lot, not least because of the reference to one of the favourite movies of me and my sons – *Cloudy with a Chance of Meatballs* – and the tongue-tied and repressed father in that story who needed a machine to make his love audible. The stage was a space for men's stories and movement, the raggedy bravado of their cockiness a front for aching tales of not being loved. As one character said: *we all hurt.* And we all need help. Sometimes.

Part IV

THE BEAUTIFUL SPOTTED BOY

George

George was barely one year old when he was taken from Saint Vincent, and he was four when the pains began in his chest and jaw. He knew his age only because the other children told him – unlike them he had no birthday celebrations where their families brought treats and candies and made small cakes and buns. There were no candles on a cake for him to falteringly count and then blow out. But they told him it had been three years that he had been with the travelling theatre, three years since its owner John Richardson had dipped his hand into his pockets to purchase George straight off the ship which carried him from the Caribbean, and then had brought him to London from the port of Bristol.

The other children played with George sometimes, if their parents let them. But the adults would stare at him, quieter than the customers who thronged to see him when the fair opened, but still as if he were alien to their world. Even the ones whose distinctive shapes and features meant they too, like George, were put on display in the sideshows. There were though a few workers and traders who saw George for all that he was, saw his dark skin (rather than the pale patches) and hair with a bounce and feel like theirs and remembered their own long journeys across the sea.

After the stalls and theatre were erected, the day's work done and the crowds had dispersed into the pitch-black night, the performers, musicians, labourers and stagehands would go back to their caravans with their wives and husbands, and they would sit and talk and fall asleep together. If they had children of their own, they would have already taken supper before the gates opened to the paying customers at six o'clock. Sometimes George could see that the man was black and the wife white, and once, when the trail of wagons passed the procession of another fair, George stared wide-eyed when he saw a couple where it was the other way round. But George had no family to go back to when darkness fell on the fair.

At first, they put him in a cage. Not out of any concern that he could escape on his infant legs into the strange and teeming city streets or onto country lanes where the hedgerows were three times as high as him. Instead, they caged George to stop any other entrepreneurial showman snatching him, and to emphasise the exoticism and wildness that they wanted even greater crowds to be drawn in by.

The punters would traipse by and stare, drunk and curious, staggering and upright, throwing pennies and blackened bananas pilfered from the docks and wharves. They would spit at him, just to see the reaction of a frightened three-year-old child. But they grew bored quickly and moved on when their friends grabbed and pulled them away to gasp and marvel at another one of the performers who they called freaks.

There was a lady whose belly was full and wide as if she had eaten too many breakfasts and dinners, but her chest and neck were as thin as those of a swan. There was a man whose beard grew all the way down to his toes so that he was always close to tripping over it, and the nails on his fingers and toes were long and gnarled, curling like the tendrils on too-old potatoes. George would share the stage sometimes with a lady who had no arms but who, aside from the help of her female companion to dress and to eat, was otherwise dependent upon nobody.

As the months passed, Richardson took George out of his cage and, to the sly-eyed bemusement of the fairhands, took him to sleep in his caravan instead, a wagon which inside, in contrast to Richardson's usual determinedly dishevelled appearance, resembled a doll's house from a children's illustrated book with snow-white curtains tied back with red ribbons, pictures illustrating Bible stories on every wall and willow-pattern china on the shelves. There was a real bird – a canary in a cage that chirped and sang and kept Richardson company before George came – and a wooden cuckoo which emerged on a spring out of a clock each hour to announce the time.

Richardson gave George a toy too, a horse on a wheel and stick which the boy could push around with excitement while the other children watched silently. But those children had so much more: they all had mothers, and some had fathers too.

In the evenings after the show had ended, Richardson sat George down, gave him an apple or orange to chew on and talked into the empty air about men with names such as Kean, Dickens and Stirling. George would nod, smile, frown and laugh, and wonder if these people were the family that everyone else in the travelling theatre seemed to have or talk about, but which Richardson had lost.

George could remember his own barely at all. As he picked up the words of the other children, George asked Richardson sometimes *where his ma and pa were, and Richardson would say that they were a long way away still in a place called Saint Vincent. He told George that they had their freedom now and were happy.*

As was usual with Richardson, he would not stop there but would go on beyond the limits of George's comprehension and say that he said he believed George's parents had been fond of him but 'natives' in the colonies had many children and for sure they could not be expected to take care of them all.

'They sent ye to me so I could make your fortune,' Richardson would boom out, waving his hands as he grew excited, his loud voice escaping the four close, wooden walls so that people passing outside would pause and stare at the faintly lit cabin.

'And along the way to make myself one too! Soon they'll stop calling me a penny showman!' Richardson would add with laughter, pinching George's cheek with a chuckle as he promised to make the child part of the greatest spectacle in the world.

Richardson let the boy sleep at the bottom of his bed on a small mattress and would cover him with a quilt which in its colours he said was like Joseph's cloak. Under it, the boy would dream. Dream and remember a different room where he could hear women cry as he snuffled against his mother's breast, their voices like an irregular rhythm, predictable at times in their beat but then falling away into scattered pinpricks of noise around him. He heard the voices even though, just like now, he could not understand them. And he could hear a noise in the background: a thud which travelled through the air and vibrated from the ground up into the bed and his soft body. It was a rhythm he felt again when he was suckled by the wet nurse in the belly of the cutter heaving its way eastwards against the Atlantic waves. A woman with three pickney of her own still clinging to her, one also still an infant, but who nonetheless was made to detach her child and to give him milk first because he was precious and valuable. A commodity. A package to be delivered safely with no more marks on his skin than those with which he was born.

Sometimes Richardson would take George by the hand as they walked down the main street of whichever shire town the company had settled upon, and the whole length of the way Richardson would talk to the child without expecting a reply in return. George could barely understand his words and had few to give back of his own. But slowly, the boy came to understand that Richardson once had a wife and a child too, a family of his own, although now they were gone.

Although his voice could be rough and his answers sharp, Richardson was kind. He would walk along in his top hat and lean on his stick, and the children of the fair chased after him as he conducted his inspections. He was quick to swear at the stagehands because of loose ropes or rubbish left lying around. But he threw the children sweets out of his pockets like the Pied Piper in the stories the Painted Lady would sometimes tell the children on the evenings when the travelling theatre had just arrived in another town and before the show opened the next day.

Richardson liked all the children, but it was only George who he kept close by him, the toddler's age and the man's slow gait meaning that the mismatched pair kept the same pace as they walked around the fairground. In the towns, sometimes they passed groups of rough boys or men, drinking out of long-necked bottles at one end of a

*local bridge, where they spat into the river or sometimes onto startled
and furious rowers below.*

*'Oi, mate, is that your pet monkey?' they might shout, jumping
up and down with arms curled beneath their shoulders.*

'Who's your nigger boy? Who's the freak?'

*Richardson would say nothing until close enough to lash out and
catch one painfully behind the ear or on the knee with his stick. And
inevitably, if it had not happened before, someone would catch the
offended ruffian by the shirt as he strode forward to take revenge
with his fists. 'Oi, oi, mate, leave it. Come away now. That's Mr
Richardson. Good evening, sir. No harm meant, sir!'*

*The theatre travelled around, competing with other companies
for the prime spots at all the fairs in and around London although
the combination of Richardson's fierce temper and famous generosity
meant that few were willing to resist him in a direct dispute about
who got to pitch where. Saint Albans, Marlow, Lady Fair in South
London, where the lights of Southwark Bridge glittered in the distance like a necklace, and May Fair where the toffs came down to get
their thrills with the hoi polloi. But the busiest and most profitable
time for the theatre was at Saint Bartholomew's Fair in Smithfield,
where the company stopped for two late weeks of summer when the
city stank, and the air hung dense in the narrow streets and lanes.
There Richardson might take over £1,000 in scarcely three days.*

*The fair was raucous and disorderly, and as many pickpockets,
thieves and confidence men flowed around the stages and stalls as
respectable patrons. Beer was cheap, and there were drunkards
aplenty, male and female, staggering from show to show or falling*

asleep against the bales of hay whose straw covered the churned-up mud and, where need be, the vomit. People who came to see the show stared through befuddled and uncaring eyes at those who had been put on display as curiosities, but also laughed and threw pebbles and dirt. Sometimes even the men who erected the stage and tents, took the money and pulled the wagons into place, joined in the jeering. They were rough and foul in their language and looked at the sideshow women in a way that made them turn away and pull their shawls tight around their shoulders.

The theatre tent itself was thirty yards long and ten yards broad with canvas doors and roof, and the stagehands had to start putting it up two days before the shows began. Draperies ran around the outside to deny the curious a view without paying. The final structure looked like a castle with turrets and pennants fluttering in the London air, as high as the trees whose tops waved in the easterly wind coming in off the river.

Outside the theatre was the platform where the night before every show all the attractions and actors paraded with clowns and trumpeters; Columbine and Harlequin; wraiths, jesters and mysteries. Before the evening's dramas were presented, Richardson would take George by the hand to that platform outside and gently ask him to stand so that the people could see him. A drummer strode about on the street and through the crowds, calling and challenging the men to come in on pain of them being called a cheapskate in front of their sweethearts if they refused to pay the one shilling it cost to see 'The Beautiful Spotted Boy, the real, live "hinfant" phenomenon!'

Inside, the theatre was ornately beautiful, with huge, red curtains falling from the highest point at the stage end. Stagehands sprang up ladders, as if the spirit of seafarers was in them, to fix the ropes and lanterns and raise the curtains.

As the audience jostled and pushed for space and air, the players strode about on stage throwing their booming voices as far back across the crowd as they could, resplendent in scarlet and gold velvet and satins. Flickering oil lamps were placed all around the stage and threw shadows onto the faces of the expectant and excited spectators. Sweet sellers in red jackets and white breeches squeezed through any small gap in the crowd – small, grey-banded hats askew and held on their heads only by the straps under their chins.

Outside the theatre, the sounds of the fair were always loud and raucous. There were musicians and tightrope walkers, puppet shows, and lions and monkeys in cages. Drummers and flute players strode about. And the sideshows were where they kept the curiosities. Dwarfs, muscle men, bearded ladies. And George.

The stagehands would dress him. Place a headdress of cord or some rough plant onto his head and tie a cloth around his loins. Put a sharp stick into his hands as if to make a spear and ask him to strike a pose like one of the warriors whose picture Richardson had seen in one of the few books he bought but could never read.

Another time they armed George with a bow and arrow like Cupid. An artist came to the theatre to paint him dressed like this. He asked George to stay still for hours while the other children whistled and laughed at him, until Richardson came to chase them away.

When they wanted George to pose as if he were an ancient Roman, his head decoration was fashioned of ivy, and they draped a robe as close to pure white as they could find over the boy's shoulders and belted it around his midriff.

The old man also liked to dress him as the Prince of Barbary or Africa, although George had no idea where these places were any more than he had knowledge of Italy or Greece. At times, Richardson would pause, caught in a recollection, and tell George that he reminded him of another man he had known from the Caribbean islands – a man he called Boby.

'Skin like yours he had, boy, but he was tall and upright and bore hisself well like a white man. I hear these days he is done with the travelling life and settled in London with a wife of his own. An Englishwoman at that.'

George might have to stand on stage in his costumes for twelve hours, and even after he was allowed to step down from the people's gaze, he still earnt Richardson money because his workers sold the crowds trinkets and mementoes engraved with George's image. Sometimes a lord or lady hearing about the Spotted Boy but not wishing to endure the smells and throng of the fair called for him to be brought to them. The boy would wait shivering in the marble-floored anterooms of grand houses in Piccadilly or Mayfair while these aristocrats walked around him, comparing their printed invites with the child before them, checking for themselves the accuracy of the description of 'the most wonderful work of God'. They peered over their spectacles, sometimes prodding him to check whether he had the power of speech or sliding their fingers across his skin to see whether his spots — 'of the most beautiful and transparent brown and white' — had been painted on as was sometimes rumoured.

George did all he could to please the elderly white gentleman who was his only protector. He posed and stood and even endured the pokes and pinches. But in the autumn of 1812, as he turned four years of age, he began to have fits when he coughed uncontrollably. When this happened, it hurt too much for him to hold back the tears, and sometimes red stains were left on the kerchief Richardson gave to him or on the straw laid on the ground where George tried to spit out the bitter taste in his mouth.

Richardson would lead George down from the stage again and let the boy wrap his arms around his neck as he took him back to his small caravan. The stagehands and would-be customers would stare at him strangely, but here, in Richardson's dominion, no one would say a word. Back in the wagon, he laid George on the mattress covered by the patchwork quilt and watched the boy until his coughing subsided and he fell asleep.

When the fair stopped in Marlow, Richardson sent for a doctor called Lipscomb. The pains in George's chest had grown and were more frequent now. The physician arrived in smart pantaloons and jacket and paused hardly at all when he stooped to enter the small caravan and saw that a young Negro boy was his patient — Richardson always paid well, and there were stranger maladies he had been called to the showgrounds to assist with.

From a briefcase at his side, he took shiny metal contraptions to listen to George's chest and look into his eyes. He knelt by the child's side and, propping the small body up, gave him a brown, tepid and *foul-smelling tea to drink — 'once a night before you sleep, young lad!' — and then shut down the door of the cabin and stood outside in the drizzle with Richardson.*

Inside, as he sweated and drifted between wakefulness and sleep, George could hear them talk but not what they said, because unusually for his conversations with another grown man, Richardson did not raise his voice above a whisper, not one single time.

Journey to Marlow

In June 2018, my mum, dad and I sat in their living room in Luton and ate fish and chips as we watched the news. Not the BBC or ITV – this time I had perched my laptop next to me on the small sofa opposite my parents' armchairs and connected it to the TV so that I could show them news from Saint Vincent. There were always items that I thought my mum and dad might sit up at, stories from back home about Vincentian politics, tourism and crime. Sometimes we watched the obituaries of people across the island who had passed away that followed after the main bulletins, national TV and radio sharing the news across communities and families.

I thought my parents would find this connection with what was happening in Saint Vincent of great interest, but they never did as much as I expected, unless they heard about someone they knew or might be related to. Perhaps this was a consequence of living more than three quarters of their lives as migrants raising a family in the UK and, despite remaining intimately connected to those they had left behind, having to focus on the practicalities of living – and surviving – in their new homeland.

That evening though, a segment with a direct link to the UK came on, and although my parents were distracted talking about something else, it grabbed my attention.

Projected on the screen was the grainy image of a child born and taken from Saint Vincent more than 200 years before. A little Black boy with white patches on his skin. His name was George Alexander Gratton. The newsreader said that George had been transported to England to be put on show. In modern times, we would now know that George had the non-contagious, non-life-threatening skin condition called vitiligo. But in Georgian England, he had been seen as a curiosity and a freak of nature. He had died at the tender age of four, and now a Vincentian community group in High Wycombe wanted to restore the grave of this boy who had been taken from the Caribbean to be put on display.

I was gripped by George's story. My laptop wobbled on the cushion of the red sofa as I shifted to get a better view of the screen. I thought about how George had been transported parentless between England and Saint Vincent, just like I had been once, although we went in opposite directions. I wondered what pressures could have forced George's mother and father to release him for such a cold purpose and remembered holding my own son for the first time and feeling his chest rise and fall within the vessel of my hands and arms.

It came back to me how scared I was and yet so happy. I cradled my son and walked him up and down the darkened ward telling him all the ways I would love him. When I remembered how bound I was to him and my own experience of childhood separation, thinking about any parent having to let go of their child was unbearable for me.

A few months later, I visited Luton again and spent the morning with my parents before packing up my car to get ready to travel south-west to Buckinghamshire.

'Bye, Mum,' I said.

'Where you going?' she asked.

'Over to High Wycombe. Well Marlow really. To see the grave of that boy from Saint Vincent.'

'Wha'? A boy die?'

'No, not now, Mum. That boy who was on the telly. He passed away a long, long time ago, in 1810 – or 1813. Something like that. He was only little. They brought him over when he was a baby.'

'Why?'

'To put him in a circus, mum. To put him on display.'

I knew that through human history, disabled people had been exhibited as objects of dread and fascination. In medieval Europe there was a well-established belief that bodily deformity was the result of sinfulness. And later, white Europeans feared that the complexion of mixed colours, which was the result of vitiligo, might have come about from what they called 'miscegenation', the mixing of races whose God-ordained paths should only touch when labour was served and labour extracted. Plantation owners, overseers and other white workers in the Caribbean and United States were notorious for the rape of enslaved women. George's removal from Saint Vincent could have been in part because of the possibility that he represented a violation of the line between owners and the owned.

Before my visit to Marlow, I tried to gather more information about George's short life. I searched the internet and followed up as much as I could with the authors of articles about George that I found. But local groups seemed to hold on to what they knew about him as if it were the location of buried treasure.

I received an email from the chair of a historical society, which started with the question: 'What can I tell you about our George?' Reading it I realised that George was still owned and still on display. Access to his story and secrets was guarded and regulated, even though George was now free of life's chains and lain to rest in the bosom of a bucolic Buckinghamshire commuter town.

Fifteen months after his birth, George was transported to Bristol on the merchant ship *Friends of Emma*. Even before George was taken from the island, the process of making money from his appearance began. Separated from his parents, in the months before the *Friends of Emma* sailed, he was exhibited in the port capital Kingstown for the price of a dollar per person, the length of viewing time unspecified in the few records that were kept of his infant life.

When he arrived in England, George came into a world already entranced by the notion of the exotic native. Years before I saw that SVGTV news item, I had visited an exhibition at the Royal College of Physicians which explored the lives of disabled people who were represented in a collection of portraits made between the seventeenth and nineteenth centuries. The portraits included a print of John Boby, who was given the exotic and romantic title *The Wonderful Spotted Indian*, although, like

George, he was from the Caribbean and was also at one time an exhibition in travelling shows. Another term of the period for both George and John Boby would have been 'pied-blacks' because of their black-and-white skin. Their appearance was well-known enough to be given a name but still could be also feared and labelled as abnormal.

Many of the other disabled people who were portrayed in the Royal College of Physicians exhibition had also been put on show to the public for commercial gain, sometimes choosing to exhibit themselves but often employed as performers in circuses and travelling shows. The focus of the collection was on how disabled people were seen as 'freaks of nature' – their lives and bodies catalogued and classified as scientific curiosities and also viewed as aberrations whose financial value could be exploited.

I was fortunate to see these paintings interpreted by disabled people and their organisations in a way which brought extra dimensions to the lives of the women, men and children shown on paper and canvas. The subjects of the paintings had worked, married, raised families and had their own place in society – sometimes, but not always, in control of their own destiny.

The pictures told another story too. Many of the subjects in the portraits were also Black, despite the prevailing narrative that Black people had not had a significant presence in this country before the twentieth century. The portraits supported other recently recognised evidence that Black people had been part of and had made a noteworthy contribution to English society for much longer than that.

George was bought for 1,000 guineas by John Richardson, a showman originally from Marlow, and put on show as a 'live curiosity piece'. Richardson's theatre travelled around southern England, stopping at the annual fairs of various country towns. Putting George on show and exhibiting him for perhaps twelve hours each day, could earn Richardson as much as £1,200 over three days – an amount which would be worth £100,000 in modern currency.

The booklet for the Royal College of Physicians exhibition noted that Boby's story appeared to have ended in relative happiness as he gained his freedom as an adult and married an Englishwoman. George's life was much shorter. He died in 1813, aged four years and nine months, after suffering 'a gathering in the jaw': a tumour or infection. George succumbed to this illness, seemingly far away from anyone who would mourn his passing. But Richardson apparently treated the boy who had been 'leased' into his care for three years with kindness and affection. According to available accounts, he treated George like a son and in 1810 had him christened at Saint Mary's Newington in South London. It was just three years later that George's funeral took place at All Saints Church, Marlow.

Richardson waited nearly three months to bury George. After years of putting the child on show, he did not want the boy's body stolen for further misuse and exposure. Richardson himself died aged seventy in November 1837. His wish had been to be buried next to George in the graveyard of All Saints. The resting place of these two souls whose lives had such different origins was where I was drawn to.

It was beautiful driving through the countryside on that summer's day, the car warmed by the sunlight which scattered through the trees as the road undulated through the Chiltern Hills. The anchors of my life had shifted significantly, and the journey brought welcome familiarity. I remembered making it as a child: Sunday afternoon drives with my family to see relatives in High Wycombe with an occasional diversion to explore Ashridge Forest. It wasn't until I was much older that I understood that it was High Wycombe that we went so often to because of the myriads of Vincentians who had settled there in the 1960s, bringing with them friendships and family relationships created far away in the Caribbean.

As soon as I found the parish church and parked, I realised my mistake in not calling ahead of my visit. There were hundreds of graves, headstones tilted as if in prayer, indistinguishable in the uniformity of their lichen-painted browns and greys and surrounded by clumps of ankle-high grass.

I could not go into the church itself because a wedding was in progress. I had to wait until the wedding party exited into the churchyard, guests magnificent in their top hats and fascinators, the happy couple starting a new passage of their life together whilst death lay all around them.

It was only when they had all moved out of the churchyard, presumably for a reception in one of the town's high-end restaurants, that someone found a helpful verger for me. While she changed from her robes into ordinary clothes, I waited in the hush of the nave and looked up at the walls where there were several paintings of George in different poses. He had variously been depicted as an African prince with spear and headdress; or Cupid-like with bow, arrow and quiver; or seated on a turtle feeding a dog, both George's naked tubby toddler body and the dog's trunks and legs patterned with the same spots and flecks of black on their pale bodies. In the portraits, George's face was either inscrutable or at most had only the hint of a smile, a band of white covering his forehead, nose and chin but not his eyes, whose gaze revealed nothing.

The verger found me and took me outside, and nearly straight away we found a place where two headstones were bracketed together. The inscriptions on the headstones were long faded and the graves unmarked in that crowded churchyard. But from my research I knew what the faint tracings on George's memorial had once said:

TO THE MEMORY OF
GEORGE ALEXANDER GRATTON
THE SPOTTED NEGRO BOY
From the Caribbe Islands, in the West Indies
A Native of the Carribee Islands, in the West Indies.
Who departed this life February 3d, 1813,
Aged four years and three quarters.
This Tomb, erected by his only Friend and Guardian,
Mr. John Richardson, of London.

Should this plain simple tomb attract thine eyes,
Stranger, as thoughtfully thou passest by,
Know that there lies beneath this humble stone,
A child of colour, haply not thine own.
His parents born of Afric's sun-burnt race,
Tho' black and white were blended in his face,
To Britain brought, which made his parents free,
And shew'd the world great Natur's prodigy.

Depriv'd of kindred that to him were dear,
He found a friendly Guardian's fost'ring care,
But, scarce had bloom'd, the fragrant flower fades,
And the lov'd infant finds an early grave,
To bury him his lov'd companions came,
And drop't choice flowers, and lis'd his early fame;
And some that lov'd him most, as if unblest,
Bedwe'd with tears the whice wreath on his breast.
But he is gone, and dwells in the abode,
Where some of every clime must joy in God!

On that sunny Buckinghamshire afternoon, I wondered
if George was watching, wondering why I had come to him.
George was a wraith now, I was sure. In the place where he was
born and where I had been a child too, they would call him
a jumbie, although here he chased no one, scared no donkeys
or small children, nor did he throw over chairs or wait by the

graveyard to make grown people run home as fast as they could past the mounds of bare brown earth and fading wreaths. Now he simply dreamt, bound close to the cold remains of the man who gave him the only affection he would ever remember after his mother had told him he was beautiful and then had to let him go. The man who bought him for 1,000 guineas and whose headstone was locked to his now forever.

Part V

SAINT VINCENT ONCE MORE

Lin

1974, Texas

She is writing a last letter to her children. Outside, taxi horns blare, and small children shrivel in the southern heat. She is in a hurry – her next shift starts in an hour, and she does not know what to say to the other nurses. Her suitcases are packed again, and her powder-blue vanity case sits on the bed ready to receive her papers and travel documents. Soon, she will take a flight even further south to get her children.

She never replied to the letter from the Department of Naturalisation. She did not mention it in any of the aerogrammes that she still posted nearly daily to Winston. It stayed stuffed in the top drawer of her bureau, still in the Manila envelope which two weeks ago she had torn open with shaking hands. She left emptying that drawer till last, but she finally pulled it fully out and placed it on the bed to go through it because it would be only a day or two before a new nurse arrived – from India, Pakistan, Australia or the UK – a woman probably almost mute with nervousness just like she had been months ago.

Now, Lin knew her own steps towards gaining citizenship in the US had ended. The dotted lines at the bottom of the single page remain unsigned – the invitation to interview unaccepted. She will go back to England, but first she has to get the children and bring them with her. Her children need her to be with them right now, and whatever dreams she and Win had for their family have to come second to that. There will be several flights via Miami, Puerto Rico and finally Barbados before she can gather them in her arms again. And be held herself by her own Mummy and sisters back in Dickson as she grieves for all that has come to pass and the future that will not.

After she has taken the children back to Dickson and their granny, there will be a longer journey back to London where Winston will be waiting for them. The United States will become a lost continent for her, its signifiers dotted like islands through her life. For years to come on trips between England and the Caribbean, she will use as hand luggage the vanity case that Nema bought her as a leaving gift on a last trip to the stores at Seminary South.

Back in Luton, their trauma receding, her children will find and play with and wonder at the watch fob which she received from the staff on West One ward at an entirely unexpected leaving party. Their small fingers will trace again and again over the inscription on the back saying 'Thank You Lin – We Will Miss You'.

But the avenues, boulevards and shopping malls of Fort Worth will become a heat-hazed memory. She will go back home to Winston, and eventually they will buy a new house, not one in the baked Texan suburbs but a semi-detached newbuild in a place called Leagrave. A neighbourhood where there are parks and space between the houses and where her walk to work takes only ten minutes. An entirely different future to the one she and Win had spent months planning for at the kitchen table in the old house.

She puts the brown envelope in her bag along with all her other papers and notebooks, and when they are finally home, and the children are settled, she will show Winston the letter. But her bags are packed again and all she has to do now is wait in the small apartment's living room for her cab to arrive.

The Iguana

In 2008, I returned to Saint Vincent to visit my parents with my own family: my partner and our two boys aged eight and four. My Vincentian relatives gathered around us – pleased to see me again and the new generation I had brought with me. I had been away a long time, and I seized as many opportunities for reconnections as I could.

My Uncle Walter and I always enjoyed a chat and a drink, and one day we arranged to meet in the local bar. Walter – wiry, thin and his body hard and weathered like the driftwood on Biabou beach – worked the land every single day, and his habit was to go up into the mountains early and then come back down mid-afternoon. We sat outside there through the afternoon, on high wooden stools, drinking beers (me) and rum (him) and watching the slow parade of villagers pass in either direction. This was where on Saturday nights people would gather to sing karaoke, but that day it was quiet, and for much of the time we said nothing at all, to each other or anyone else. Hanging out together was enough.

It was some time before I noticed the bag bundled and tied up at my uncle's feet. I thought it contained Walter's dirty farming clothes, but then I saw that the bag had a slow shuffle and movement of its own, as if something lay coiled within.

Walter wobbled on his seat when I asked him what it was, and I thought he was going to fall off as he tried to lean down to open the bag without getting off his stool. He loosened the ties just a little to create a small, dark O, but as my eyes acclimatised, I could see the slither of green and a baleful amber eye staring back at me.

'Iguana,' he told me.

'Why you have an iguana in your bag?'

'Fuh eat it nah!'

Just then a sergeant from the police station up the hill passed down the road on a stroll, nodding but definitely not smiling at anyone who caught his eye.

In Saint Vincent, the way people responded to the letter of the law could be confusing. Many things were done on an easy come, easy go basis: drinking a beer as you drove along the coast might be nothing more than a sign that you were chilled, and out in the villages everyone smiled indulgently at our 'English' habit of locking in our seat belts when we got in a car. But on a drive into Kingstown, as soon as the outskirts of the capital were reached, where constables might be patrolling on foot or in their cars, the straps would be pulled across shoulders and chests. No one wanted to mess with the stern authority of the police or to end up sweating in front of a magistrate at the Central Court.

Strict rules were already in place back then to enforce the protection and conservation of wildlife. Although previous generations had for centuries taken freely of both the flora and fauna of the island, I knew that these days the dwindling iguana population was definitely off the menu.

I hushed my uncle with a short, sharp whisper and jerked my head in the direction of the passing police officer. My uncle shot himself upright with an alertness exaggerated by the drink in him, and his dangling foot kicked the bag as he tried to place it on the bar of the footstool. The lizard, already excited by its brief glimpse of sunlight, thrashed around, and the bag heaved and bubbled demonically. I held my breath and wondered about what would happen next, how the officer would cuss us out in front of everyone and where I would be able to find the money for the inevitable fine as I had nearly reached the end of both my holiday and my funds.

But someone called out to the officer from the bar on the other side of the road, and with his attention distracted, my uncle was able to tie the bag up tightly and stash it behind the open door beside us and out of sight.

The next day my boys were introduced to the iguana. Its dark, banded tail tapered to a thin point like a waiting whiplash, double the length of the green, thick stump of a body which was speckled with yellow. From snout to tail tip, the whole animal was longer than my youngest boy. A frill of spines ran the length of its back, a reminder of its prehistoric lineage.

Despite its agitation the previous day, the iguana now lay passively in their arms, which had to be outstretched to the max, amazement and just a little fear in their eyes. I did not have the heart to tell them we were going to eat it.

Later, I picked through the bones of the stew my uncle had made. As he had told me, the meat itself did indeed taste like chicken, but the floating slices of still faintly patterned skin in the broth reminded me that what we were eating was reptilian, and going forward, these animals were unlikely to need much protecting from me.

A few days later, my parents took us all for a day out at Rawacou, which was fifteen minutes' drive or so south of Biabou on the windward coast. Family friends came with us, and uncles and aunties so that in total our party must have numbered more than twenty. My sons ran around with other local children, a hurtling gaggle of screams, bare arms and legs, T-shirts and shorts getting ever dirtier through whichever games they exchanged and taught each other. Callaloo and curry goat bubbled in pots on an outdoor grill; my father had asked for a goat to be killed because this was a special occasion. Rawacou felt like a secret wilderness with the view of the sea, waves and palm trees, and stretches of grass large enough for picnics to be laid out and barbeques roasted as picnickers played, limed and relaxed together.

Beyond the palms was a large, jaggedly circular natural bathing pool fed by seawater where people went to bathe. It was deep enough for my adventurous small boys to know that they were swimming, but shallow enough for me to wade across, taking care not to lose my footing. At the far end, the sea which my mother always feared would whip us away at Biabou now had its leaps cut low by a sea wall of slippery rocks, while at the front, a small cliff of stone and boulders dropped down the leisure area above. That natural but safe sea pond was a magnet for the children who jumped in and out like seal pups under my watchful supervision.

When the boys and other children had tired and returned up top from splashing, I needed a pee; I slid into the water again and, staying close to the rockface, sidled around to a place where I thought I was out of view. The stream escaped my body like an amber sigh spattering the rocks and salt water.

And then I heard a voice: 'Eh, Monty, yuh ah enjoy the water eh. Yuh tek a little sea bath?'

My neck and head shot up, and there above me I could see my aunty Joan, her broad face smiling jovially as she sipped at the bottle of Hairoun she held in one hand. She wore a striped green-and-white blouse and a faded brown cap with an N and a Y intertwined on it, and she peered over her glasses as she looked down at me. Clearly, only my head and shoulders were visible as I tried to press against the rocks because she showed no sign of knowing what I was up to.

Immediately, all of me froze, and inside the flow of liquid became immobile, paused in time – it felt as if it was perhaps even moving backwards towards my kidneys. Whether out of embarrassment at the thought of being caught peeing in such an idyllic location or because I felt too exposed, I did not want Joan to find out what I was up to. Joan was very loud and a joker, and I knew that if she realised what was happening, she would raise her voice not lower it, and her laughter and teasing would bring an even bigger audience over.

'Yes,' I grunted, a half grin fixed upon my face because I knew if my face relaxed, my sphincter would too, and I would wet my swimming trunks very visibly. 'Yes, it is nice, isn't it? Lovely place. Beautiful.'

Then there was a pause during which I expected Joan to amble back to the tables around which everyone else was sitting, kids on the grass, elders on their folding chairs. I waited and then realised that Joan was looking out to sea as if for a sailing ship to appear that she had expected days ago. Internally, my pelvic muscles gave a twitch as they struggled to dam the reservoir inside me. And yet still Joan would not leave.

I forced out some other words through a grimaced smile: 'Hey, what the others up to?'

Joan twisted her neck back to look at the crowd, but then, instead of strolling back in that direction, proceeded to give me a person-by-person description of what everyone was doing. I knew now that I had only a few seconds before I would have to relieve myself. I thought about swimming away, but it was so shallow that there was barely enough water to dive into without walking a distance I felt incapable of right then. So I closed my eyes, gritted my teeth, gave an internal heave and made the desire to pee go away. Or at least it subsided for a while until finally the smell of roast breadfruit drew Aunty Joan away and I could finish my business.

The chat that afternoon was warm and convivial, and later I sat on a folding chair between Joan and Walter, and they told me again how they remembered me on the island when I was a young boy only a little older than my eldest. A man called Pablo who I did not recognise came over to tell me that I used to beat him up when we were little, something that I remembered not at all, but he was smiling and shook my hand.

As the sun disappeared over the mountains and the air cooled, we got up to go, and everyone trundled the leftovers and rubbish into big, black plastic bags. When we filled up the boots of our cars, I noticed how some people simply flung their rubbish bags into gullies behind some bushes nearby. This lack of care conflicted wildly with the quiet custodianship that people exercised in growing the bountiful crops, from pineapples to marijuana, that the island could produce. It astounded me that people could spoil the beauty of such a place so casually, but it was something I had noticed before. Which is not to say that there was no respect for the natural environment. It was just that rules and regulations needed to compete or lie in tension with local custom, culture and tradition.

On Saint Vincent, wildlife such as turtles, manicou and agouti were still seen as local treats and prey. It did not happen often, but older locals at Biabou still remembered and spoke about eating the prize of the flesh of the sea turtles which had battled through the tumultuous waves each year to lay their eggs on the beach. However, there were strict rules about what could be hunted and when and how much of it.

Saint Vincent still fiercely held on to its international whaling quota argued for and granted in recognition of the history and social significance of the practice on Bequia, the largest and closest Grenadine Island, also citing the contribution of meat and fat to the diet of the island's inhabitants. Every year, after being blessed, the remaining couple of sailboats were allowed to try to catch up to four humpback whales, although years could go by without any being harpooned. Walter had not been completely out of step trying to eat iguana – he just did it at the wrong time and outside the rules.

I had mixed emotions as I noted how casual people could still be about dumping their garbage on this stunningly beautiful island. I rationalised it by thinking about the priorities and pressures that I thought most ordinary people had to manage. Saint Vincent was breathtakingly picturesque, but it was also hard work to navigate the main island, and back then there were few of the income-generation opportunities or the passion for tourism and keeping beaches and beauty spots pristine that I had seen in Aotearoa, Barbados or on the southerly Grenadine Islands that were the haunts of well-off yachties. People here, including those closest to me, had to concentrate on finding ways to survive and make a living, and sometimes the environment was simply not top of their priorities.

But family always was. As people packed up cool bags and climbed into cars, I looked around and felt overwhelming happiness as I saw family and friends, and kith and kin from across the decades and born on different islands tidying up, all of whom had taken different journeys to be here on our island.

Later that night, I felt a stabbing pain in my abdomen, and despite repeated visits to the toilet, I could not go, no matter how much I willed my bladder to again empty. When my mother and father took me to a doctor up the road from Biabou the next day to treat me, I was exhausted and suffering. I felt like a schoolchild – instead of me taking care of my own children, my parents were still taking care of me. But somehow it did not seem to matter that I was leaning back into their love again, no matter what age I was or where we were in the world, as long as we were together.

There was a time when I had wondered whether it would be possible for me to come back, whether I would fit in again or if the good parts of what I thought I remembered had ever really existed. Now I knew that 'mi nah hafi drop bone to chase shadow' as the old Vincentian phrase went. Everything I needed was already touching my skin and heart and had always been. There was nothing more to find, and it was alright for us to be who we wanted to be even if others withheld their permissions. I knew now that the ancestors would hold us through all our incarnations.

Nightingale

October 2018

Our flight landed in Saint Vincent on a moonlit night, the earth's companion floating in the sky like a fecund gourd. The sea was black, the path of light laid across the waves not disrupted into shards but shimmering. As we stepped down from the plane and walked across the tarmac to the new airport terminal at Argyle, the humid air was still welded to the hills, and the palm trees did not sway but either stood stiffly to attention or leant down to the ground doubled over with exhaustion.

It was the first time I had flown into Saint Vincent at night, and on the drive to Biabou, darkness seemed to accentuate rather than hide the dilapidation of some houses in the roadside villages. It was a big contrast to the relative prosperity of Barbados, where we had taken off from two hours before. I had never been to Africa, and I knew that in Saint Vincent no one would ever suffer hunger and death in the ways people did there. But I could feel spirits from that continent hiding in the darkness and watching the end of my mother's journey home. In their whispers, they reminded me that for every kidnapped African who was enslaved and transported to America, twelve were sent to the Caribbean. And of those who escaped, some found their freedom again on this island.

We spent a few days settling in at my parents' house which my father had called 'Nightingale'. On the kitchen wall above a cabinet of china and ornaments, hung the text of a U.A. Fanthorpe poem, 'Idyll', which years before I had shared with my father and which he loved. A friend had reproduced the poem in exquisite calligraphy for me as a gift for my parents, and I asked her to change the words of one line so that instead of naming blackbirds it read, 'There will be nightingales, in a late March evening.'

After our suitcases were unpacked and the various items we had brought over for people had been distributed, we took a family trip to the north of the island where my mother had been born. She and I sat on the back seat behind my father and brother, and we talked while my brother concentrated on the curves and bends of the road and my father called out the names of places he remembered, and the people he knew who lived in certain houses and villages. At Colonarie (which locals pronounced 'Connery'), we stopped in front of the dark eye of the Black Point 'undermile' that had been excavated by slaves in 1815 and through which the road threaded, wide enough for only one vehicle. We all got out of the car to see if we could see Saint Lucia to the north, but all that was visible was cloud and the always-blue sea.

As the little jeep struggled to climb the steep hills, my mother told us about her adventures before she first left Saint Vincent. She told us how she had climbed the volcano four times (as a man in my fifties, I had managed it once) and about how fast she could run when she was young. She was small then – she still looked small now next to the height of my father – and light on her feet and could outrun all the boys in Dickson village, competing in parish and island athletics competitions for her school.

My mother explained how, like many bright teenagers, she began training as a teacher early, Saint Vincent growing its own educators as the Crown would not send them out to the reaches of its empire. At fifteen, as a probationary assistant she was teaching children only a few years younger than her the rigorous curriculum of arithmetic, English and history lessons, the last always focused on British battles and English kings and queens. Her days were spent chiding and cajoling groups of children through their ABCs and multiplication tables, in separate corners of the single, wide-open classroom, hot air streaming in through the wooden window slats and open doors.

Her first placement as a student teacher was at South Rivers, which she had to walk to every day, five miles each way. She left home at six o'clock as the cocks crowed to get to school for eight, and if she was late, she would run, skipping in her neat pinafore past men on their way up to the mountains or weaving through meandering gangs of goats. Her black shoes were always smart and clean, but they would never last long because of the wear and tear they took. She had to make sure to save something out of her twenty dollars a month stipend to get the regular replacements that she needed.

As we drove, my mother showed me a small scar on her forehead which I had never thought to ask about. Once, after she told off a group of rowdy boys in class, they lay in wait for my mother and her friend Dorothea, and in revenge pelted them with stones from the cover of the bushes. My mother and Dorothea picked up their feet and fled as fast as they could, but still one of the stones thumped into my mother's temple and split the skin so that it needed stitches. The boys must have thought they had got away scot-free, but the young women recognised the voices that had produced the shouts and giggles, and the next day the headteacher showed the boys that some hard 'licks' with his leather strap were much worse than a telling-off.

Further on at New Grounds, my mother pointed out to us the small primary school where she worked in her last teaching role before her family saved the money to send her overseas. She had decided to change her profession and to try to qualify as a nurse in what was then the still young and radically innovative National Health Service in England. She packed her suitcase and pillow and set sail for a training placement in North London to pursue her ambitions of respectability and success.

Later that evening, after we had returned to my parents' house, I sifted through the cupboards of the tall, stately cabinet which my parents had managed to ship over to their living room in Saint Vincent, and whose glass-fronted side compartments held glasses etched with colourful fruit and birds. In and on it I found other mementoes and documents of our life as a family in England.

An ashtray from Rouen where I went to on my first-ever school trip to mainland Europe, and a wooden pipe from a residential trip in Snowdonia: curious mementoes because neither of my parents smoked, and it was not a habit that I was ever tempted by. Another small statuette was from Wolfsburg, Germany, the crossed sticks celebrating a school hockey tour. One drawer was stuffed full of papers: old school reports for me and my siblings, hymn sheets and funeral pamphlets from Methodist churches back in Luton and here in Biabou, land registry and valuation documents for the house my parents had built under the Caribbean sun. And a green-and-yellow leaflet advertising the departure dates and discounts for a shipping service between Europe and the Caribbean, taking the produce of Saint Vincent one way and ferrying back the barrels sent home by the diaspora in England. The same shipping line that my mum and dad used at the end of their visits back to the UK when they took the opportunity of lower British prices to fill a couple of barrels and then to race by plane to get back before them to Biabou.

Once the barrels arrived, my parents and a small group of family would unpack all the goods which were too expensive to buy or hard to find in the capital Kingstown and too heavy to waste airline baggage allowance on: clothes, batteries, bulbs, cleaning products. Carefully chosen paint and random toiletries and toothbrushes which had been on offer. Sometimes multipacks of Guinness and cider. Always at least a couple of bottles of Famous Grouse whisky smothered in bubble wrap for my dad to impress his friends with. The small portable radio that I remembered fighting to find a last rectangle of space for inside the barrels and which my dad now listened to when he sat in the shade under the carport. Seeing it again back in Saint Vincent reminded me of a small red radio I had there as a child and which I used to listen to the World Service in the darkness, trying to make sure that neither its tinny sounds nor my tears woke anyone.

A few years before I had visited at the Geffrye Museum in Hackney an installation called the *West Indian Front Room* created by Michael McMillan, an artist and writer of Vincentian heritage. Amongst those anodyne displays of domestic interiors through the centuries, Michael had brought together all the essence and vitality of a post-Windrush Caribbean migrant home. Bajans, Jamaicans, Vincys… any small or big islander could step through the hushed halls, pause in front of the roped-off enclosure and recognise the essential elements of their arrival, settlement or childhood in the UK. Whether now living in Tottenham, Brixton, Reading, High Wycombe, Reading, Luton or as far from London as Bristol, Cornwall and Leeds, it didn't matter – people from Black communities in all these places would recognise the room their mum and dads saved for Sundays and special occasions.

Back in Biabou, it was as if my mother and father, on retirement to the Caribbean, had decided to recreate the front room they had back in Luton. They had shipped most parts of that beautiful room back to Saint Vincent.

As well as the room-dominating, dark wooden cabinet, there was their precious stereo unit and record player, and a huge, double-tiered, glass coffee table on which angled cardboard-framed photographs jostled with china ornaments. Many of the photos were of my sons at various stages of toddlerhood or in school uniform: leaning unsteadily on a table for support, wobbling on a tricycle but kept safe by my hand behind them, or grinning into the school photographer's camera against a light-blue background. I wondered if in their sleep 4,000 miles away, they might sense that their growth and maturation had been carried away by their grandparents and now filled a Caribbean living room – whether they knew that even at that distance they were still adored.

A row of books stood at the back of the large, middle level of the cabinet. It included a dictionary whose back pages held a compendium of national flags which I used to pore over. Our mother's nursing books – which as children gripped my brother, sister and I with a morbid fascination – were there too. The diagrams of the human body, lesions and skin conditions were particularly mesmerising for us. Most of the photographs were in colour, but some of the black-and-white photography showed people with the distinct varied pigmentation of vitiligo, reduced to two tones and dimensions only. Now those medical texts stared out at me again, but I knew that was not how I wanted to look at people's bodies now.

Some of the other books were ones whose arrival I had waited for with excitement each week after hours thumbing through the pages of my school book-club catalogue and making my choices. The records stacked under the turntable also had a mix

of original owners. Many of them were the staples my parents
had played every Sunday afternoon when friends dropped in,
often unannounced, my mother cooking enough for whoever
might turn up for chicken, rice and peas or soup. On those
days, there would be a crew of adults in the front room, mostly
but not only men, laughing and joking, glasses, ice and bottles
of rum and whiskey tinkling as the record player spun reggae
45s imploring 'Oh Margaret', 'Everything I Own', 'Have a
Little Faith', 'I Can See Clearly Now' and 'Groovin' Out on
Life'. I loved watching the spiky, star-shaped inserts circling in
the middle of the record deck underneath the symbol of their
label. Trojan, Motown, Atlantic, Embassy, Columbia, Capitol,
Island – each of the names conjuring the power and mystery
of unfamiliar places.

Among the LPs, The Mighty Sparrow, the legendary calypso-
nian, filled and dominated a record sleeve, in a black suit against
a red background, legs astride his guitar. When I flicked to the
next album, Pat Boone looked back at me from the comforting
depths of his cardigan. Amongst the singles, Acker Bilk and
Fats Domino were shoulder to shoulder with Hot Chocolate
and Captain & Tennille. Somehow my single by The Kids from
Fame had crept in as had 'Karma Chameleon'. A Bananarama
record that my sister and I always fought over was tucked in
there, and Bob Marley's 'Survival' had returned to the Caribbean
to be closer to its creator's birthplace.

Buried beneath invoices and deeds in a drawer, I found a
small notebook with a faint, faded pattern of thin, squiggly

lines across its brown cover, its spine bound with blue tape. The words 'Pupil Midwives Record Book' ran along a label on the front cover. In it, I saw how hard my mother had studied and worked to earn her new career in England. How day after day she had recorded her notes of dozens of births: length of labour, dates, weights and delays.

Behind those facts and observations lay the complications, happiness and heartbreak for individual women, families and the children who they wanted to bring into the world. Within the pages were words and language some of which I thought I knew the meaning of but others used in a way which I had not seen before. 'Remarks', 'condition', 'presentation', 'position' – and 'parity', which I found out meant the number of births that a woman has had after at least twenty-four weeks gestation. A dull, flat number, recording events but unable to look into the future and see whether life and circumstance would allow those children and their mother to stay and grow together.

I wondered if George Alexander Gratton's mother had brought other children into the world and whether that helped her survive the pain of losing him. Whether if, like my mother, the path of Catherine's life was shaped not only by having children but also by the experience of separation from them.

My unanswered questions swirled and dipped like near-invisible birds in a darkening sky. Did George's mother ever hear of what became of her baby born with the black-and-white skin? Did she mourn him on that North Windward coast, even while her other children tugged at her dress and jostled for attention? Or did her newly earnt freedom mean it was all the more quick for her to forget the ache in her arms and the tenderness in her breasts?

Perhaps terse letters in elegant script came back to the island on a mail boat saying where he was and how he was famous and that she need not worry herself or enquire further. Informed her that he was now safe in England and that she would not see him again.

I wanted to reverse time so that they were both back in their village at a point before George was taken away, able to find escape before white men came in search of this strange infant they had heard rumours of. Or if as was likely, my wish had no power, for the souls of George and his mother to be back together now amongst all the other sprits who filled the forests and coasts of this island.

November 2018

My mum and I sat on the black sofa in my one-bedroom flat in Hornsey with fish and chips from the shop over the road on our laps, watching the news. I did not tell her how much a takeaway cost in North London – even minor things stressed her now, and we both needed calm after the physical and emotional journeys of the last few months, the most recent one the drive down from Luton through London rush-hour traffic. Now we planned an early night before the day of pre-op assessments she would start at the Royal Free Hospital in the morning.

As we ate quietly together, the television ran through the day's news. A war in another country, a major accident in this one. Celebrity deaths and share-price falls. And then the last item – an in-depth analysis explaining that the latest statistics on early diagnoses and effective treatment of cancer were the worst they had been for a decade.

December 2018

Soon after our return from Saint Vincent, when surgery was ruled out and after complications arose for her planned treatment, my mother decided to abandon the course of chemotherapy which she had expected to start. The consultant gave my mother the choice of going ahead if she really wanted to, but the doctor's recommendation was that she should enjoy the quality of life she still had and deal with any symptoms as and when they arrived. There would be no more follow-up appointments unless necessary, or more treks down the M1 for scans, scopes and procedures, no more hard, grey chairs to sit on under the sharp glint of waiting-room lights. Just the chance to live out her last few months with her boy from Saint Vincent and the children and grandchildren that they had brought into this world.

Mum kept asking the doctor what they thought was best, but when she found out what risks further procedures and invasions on her body carried, she decided not to go ahead. The cancer had gone too far. Now she just wanted us all to be together as a family, and that is all that we wanted too.

Because an appointment had been due the following day, I still travelled to Luton to stay with my mother and father that night. I arrived at the Hightown terrace in the middle of the evening and brought my little rucksack into the front room. My dad was already getting ready for bed next door; my parents used the back room as a bedroom because he could no longer manage the stairs, so my mum and I could hear his quiet preparations behind us as we chatted in the front room. The sounds of Dad laying out his night-time essentials – book, word search, glasses – punctuated our conversation as we sat in the dim living-room light. We talked a little about the day she had endured. My mother was upset and angry at the length of time she had to wait for diagnosis and the repeated delays she had experienced. She did not understand why things were not made clear to her earlier, although I did believe that the doctors had tried to explain in the very best way that they could.

Our mood was brightened a little when a preview came up on the flickering television for forthcoming episodes of *Strictly Come Dancing*. Since the summer, *Strictly* had given me an alternative focus during that dismal year. A friend had placed a bet for me on Stacey Dooley, the TV presenter, winning the whole competition with her professional coach and dance partner, Kevin Clifton. I knew nothing about her dance ability, and in the few early rounds I watched, Stacey and Kevin did not impress as the best combination. But I had chosen her as my bet because she was from Luton, where I had grown up, and her story of defying stereotypes about the town, plucked from shop-girl obscurity to prime-time prominence, made me a fan of hers.

I had never diligently watched *Strictly* before, but the mix of styles and abilities in the body of contestants was gripping. This was not a long-established company of dancers who trained with each other day after day, year after year. The dancers were strangers to each other, although that unfamiliarity did not last long as they were thrown together to practise contortions which one half of the coupled bodies must barely have known before. Their challenge was not just from other contestants, it was also from all the inner voices begging them to keep their limitations hidden. Despite never paying attention to *Strictly* before that series, now I watched each Saturday and Sunday as if I had a bet on the favourite for the Grand National.

Stacey Dooley's face flashed up on screen and I told my mother that I had a £10 bet on her which could win me £120. My mother, whilst not that interested in *Strictly*, asked who she was. I explained that Stacey Dooley was a young woman from the town who had gone on to make it as a TV presenter. I said that now she was famous and a contender to take home the Strictly Glitterball Trophy. That she was Lutonian and used to shop at the Arndale and get books out of the Central Library just like us.

My mother stayed with me, and as she listened, she smiled, a smile which lit her face up on that chilly night while the November wind howled outside and the sky begged the gale to let it snow.

'She's done well then. Her family must be so proud. She must win now, no?'

My mother was proud of Stacey too. Just as she was proud of Princess Diana for 'learning sign language', which infuriatingly was how my mum labelled Princess Di's faltering attempts at finger spelling. But with Stacey it went deeper – she was a Luton girl made good, and that meant so much to my mum. That and the possibility that she might have helped to deliver her into this world or met her mother ('What's her family name you say? Dooley?'). She was impressed and full of pride because Stacey was from Luton.

I nearly confessed that I had come close to cashing in my summertime bet on her a few weeks before when I would have been guaranteed modest winnings which I could secure in my wallet. But I was unable to do it – either to give up on Stacey or to tell my mother that I had wobbled. I did not want to let either of them down.

I think my mum liked Stacey because she saw that she had taken huge steps and because, like Stacey, no one would ever really understand how far my mum had travelled. How many miles she had conquered and how many summits. She had undertaken a glorious journey, a quest more intrepid than many men could dream of, more courageous than most would commit to. For love of her family, her children and her boy from Saint Vincent. She and thousands of her generation had arrived in this country to find the label 'immigrant' or 'migrant' attached to them like a dirty word, as if they had come simply to take and receive. But her generation and the travellers who came after were characterised by their desire to give and to serve – in my mother's case, through service in the NHS across four decades.

Even when she stopped working and went back to the Caribbean, her love for this country was unending. Yes, her bond with Saint Vincent where she returned home with our dad was unbreakable. But her love and commitment to the friends and neighbours she had made in this country where she had raised her family were also wide and deep. It was when I saw her smiling as she thought about Stacey Dooley that I knew that my mother – for all her travels across the ocean, from Dickson to London, from Bedfordshire to Fort Worth and back again – had been a Luton girl ever since she first came here and would remain so all her life. A life which came to an end a few weeks later on 25 December when my mother passed away in the bedroom next door, ten days after Stacey and Kevin were crowned *Strictly Come Dancing* Champions 2018.

December 2019

I stood beside Mum's grave and lit a candle. It was hard to find a way to balance it upright, but I managed it using stones and a discarded jar. Mum's grave was still unadorned while we waited the requisite months for the clinging soil to settle and be ready to receive her headstone. Only a wooden cross with a small golden plaque marked her resting place. Somehow, I think she would have liked the simplicity.

I stood quietly with my mother and told her about all that was happening in my life. I said Merry Christmas as well to her neighbours Stanley and Mildred, whose graves were untended and flowerless. There were no visitors for them that day, but I chatted with them as well. It was not All Hallows, but it felt like a day when all the ones we had lost needed to be remembered.

When my eldest child was born, I walked back down a scruffy Hackney street as if for the first time. I passed Solly's bike shop and Sim's launderette and cafés whose owners and workers had become my friends, telling all of them my news. I had made that place my home. On that morning, I wanted everyone to know that I now had a child to mark my passage in this world. He had been born in the same borough of London where my mother and father had been married more than thirty years before, where they had made their first home and had brought me into the world.

A few hours earlier, on a ward less than a mile from where she had given birth to me, my mother, with all her years of training and instinct, had carefully wrapped her new grandson tightly in a blanket, swaddled with tenderness, while his mother and I watched unsure and unknowing. I was heading home to shower and make calls, but the main thing I wanted to do was announce to the world that our family's love had found a new receptacle and our line would continue.

Now my son was a teenager, and years later I knelt at my mother's graveside feeling that my life was filled with sadness and washed bare by the tears of all my separations and losses.

I floated between worlds, not knowing where I was allowed to land.

A procession of cars for another funeral passed by, and the interruption to my reverie let in the reminder of cold winter air on my face. As my father had taught me, I picked up a stray green leaf flying on the grass, and holding it up between finger and thumb, I let the winter breeze take it and carry it away, fluttering over Mum's headstone and away across the graves as I whispered, 'I love you'. I watched Mum's candle flicker, and I promised her that I would look after her grandchildren all my life and that her family would remain strong and stay close to each other.

Neighbour

My father gave me my tasks. He stood in the middle of the kitchen, leaning on his walking stick like a general amongst his troops, although it was only I who bustled from fridge to countertop and from sink to cooker. He stood tall in his loose, short-sleeved shirt, which he thought strikingly smart with its pattern of hibiscus flowers bright over brown and red squares, baggy blue shorts with a white trim flapping around his thin legs and his red baseball cap labelled 'Simply The Best' atop his head, although we were inside. For this day of rest here in the Caribbean, Dad was dressed to both relax and impress, although there was little respite for me, and his presence and authority commanded the room.

Dad turned as he spoke to me, peering over the spectacles perched on his nose, keeping an eye on what I was doing or not doing quickly enough. He had decided to cook, and that this late October Sunday in Biabou, this would be his mission. Although most of the physical tasks would fall on my shoulders, he would direct, give orders and take credit.

Back in Luton when my brother, sister and I were children, my dad used to take over the kitchen like this on the days when he decided to treat us to his speciality of beef with Guinness (in the stew), carrots and onion. Our mum would be hustled out of the kitchen, and it would become his kingdom and his alone.

This Sunday was another of those special days. It was 27
October, the anniversary of the date that Saint Vincent became
politically independent of Britain in 1979. Our father, although
not particularly a historian, was today as regal and authorita-
tive as Chatoyer, who 200 years before had ruled the forests of
Saint Vincent in defiance of the British. Chatoyer had led the
Garinagu – the folk who had come into existence through the
mixing of Kalinago tribes, whose ancestors had over centuries
migrated northwards to the Caribbean from South America,
and people of Black African origin.

How the indigenous Kalinago had come into contact with
those Africans was disputed. One theory was that in the 1600s,
a ship transporting enslaved captives from West Africa to the
Americas sank close to the coast of Saint Vincent. Some of the
captives who survived or escaped were able to reach Bequia, the
largest and closest of the islands neighbouring Saint Vincent,
and from there were taken by the Kalinago to Saint Vincent
itself. The Africans learnt the language and customs of the
Kalinago and formed unions with Kalinago women, and it was
this intermingling that created the Garinagu who were called
Black Caribs by Europeans during their attempts to conquer
the island. But another story gave more credence to the agency
and enterprise of Black Africans from what is now Mali, who
in 1311 were said to have travelled across the Atlantic on the
equatorial current in an expedition of 2,000 ships.

However it came about, the African influence on Saint
Vincent was undisputed. During their centuries of resistance,

the Kalinago were joined by escapees from other Caribbean islands. Enslaved people in Barbados discovered that a boat or even a raft drifting westwards would end up in Saint Vincent, and those held in slavery in Saint Lucia noted how quickly Carib canoes covered the twenty-eight miles between the two islands, and also used these as a way to flee. The ferocity of the region's storms played a part too – some Africans whose transports were shipwrecked survived their incarceration below decks to reach Saint Vincent and join forces with indigenous people.

The origins of the name of Biabou itself traced back to a tribe of Caribs called the Bayabous who were forced to flee the conquered island of Guadeloupe and who then found their way to this bay on the east coast of Saint Vincent. This spirit and heritage of resistance meant that, although elsewhere in the Caribbean the enslavement of Africans lasted for over 200 years, in Saint Vincent it was in place for less than eighty. Vincentians in general, and people in Biabou specifically, did not accept any attempt to dominate them easily.

For nearly 500 years after the first contact with Europeans, the Kalinago and Garinagu continued to fiercely fight colonisation and encroachment on their homeland until 1796 after Chatoyer had finally fallen in battle in March of the previous year on Dorsetshire Hill. That hill overlooks the sea, but all the cannons placed by the British faced inland because the threat came from the Garinagu and Kalinago, who sought to drive the Europeans off the island. Chatoyer had fiercely defended the indigenous people of this island before their right to rule themselves was stolen. But now the reclamation of that self-determination was fervently celebrated and was especially so today: Independence Day.

His excitement building over the days beforehand, my father had told me that we were going to make fungee and bhaji. These were not words or dishes I had ever heard about back in the UK, but now he had returned home my father wanted to recreate a Vincentian dish of his youth.

We started by gathering our utensils and cooking ingredients, and in my contribution to getting organised, I tried to pull out everything I thought we would need. That was not easy because the contents of the drawers and cupboards had lost the order they might have had when my mother and father first moved back to the Caribbean. Knives and forks jostled with wooden spoons and ladles, and I had to reach back into the darkness of the cupboards under the sink to find the right-sized pots and pans. Jars and containers had lost their labels, and herbs and spices were in unmarked bags, but by looking, smelling and guessing, we found all the ingredients we would need.

I lined up everything along the kitchen counter to help with my own uncertainty. A dusty bag of starch and a clear plastic one straining with freshly ground coconut, black flecks buried in its paleness. Green tendrils of chives dangled over the edge of the counter, their long leaves hanging like verdant dreadlocks, and a white kitchen bowl was filled with dark-shelled freshwater shrimp collected from the bend of a river at the bottom of the inland mountains. Fat and prehistoric, they lay overturned and still like

larger-than-life woodlice. Two pans were placed on the hobs of
the cooker – one low, dull and heavy; the other upright, silver
and shiny. Only when all these were laid out did I think we were
ready, although my father was impatient with my slow orderliness.

We started with the coconut, washing the heavy handfuls in
a pot of water and then straining it through a sieve, not for the
wet coconut chaff itself, which we discarded afterwards, but for
the flavoured water that came through. I squeezed the grey liquid
out of the coconut with my fingers, the remnants sticking to my
hand like a strange second skin. Then, still entirely under orders,
I chopped the pointed green fingers of okra and combined them
in the heavy-bottomed pot with the milky water.

'Do this. Move that. Pick up that pot nuh! Bring it here!' My
father pirouetted majestically on his stick in the centre of the
kitchen as if imagining that by doing so he could simultaneously
bring several versions of me into life.

I added the shrimp, and we heated the pot to a boil and then
a simmer. I used a wooden spoon to mash the okra, the pink
seeds popping out as I crushed the softened tubes against the
wall of the pot.

While the broth of shrimp and vegetables cooked, we turned
our attention to making the fungee. Now my father insisted on
lending a hand, and he reiterated the instructions he had given
me very specifically before we started.

'Yuh grin' your arrowroot starch until it's fine, yuh boil yuh
water wi' a little salt while the water is boiling an' yuh add the
starch little by little until yuh have the amount yuh want. It

will tek two ah we, one to spin and one to pour at the same time. We hafi keep spinning until it cooks – will tek about ten minutes. Mek sure yuh nah burn de starch!'

Near us on the countertop, a bottle of Famous Grouse whisky nestled against the bag of starch, not to whet the thirst of the visitors who passed by but as a treat for the chefs, and we made sure to reward ourselves frequently. And as we cooked, people were calling in throughout, with additional refreshments of cherry juice and rum punch. Even my uncle called on his way back down from working up mountain on my dad's plot, wellingtons and clothes caked with mud, cutlass hanging at his side and his hands full with two huge cocoa pods, ridged and yellow, looking in their gravid, alien heaviness as if they had come from a Hollywood film set. Finally, one of the village elder ladies brought us dukana. These were parcels of dark green sweetness tied with a precise cross of yellow string – sweet potato and coconut baked in banana leaves. As we cooked and toiled, Biabou made sure to nourish us.

And so we set off, me starting by pouring while my dad stirred the slowly thickening liquid. Eventually we swapped when the resistance he met was too much for the waning strength in his right hand, but he could still hold the diminishing weight of the bag of starch. We then added the chives, cut into inch-long pieces, to the hot water with a splash of oil and garlic, and powdered in a Maggi's chicken bouillon cube, a local favourite ingredient. A last addition was a whole chilli from my father's little kitchen garden round the back of the house where he had planted the vegetable seeds which we brought over to remind him of the life he had made back in England.

My dad enjoyed cooking because he loved creating in all sorts of ways and he was a maker. As a young man, he had wanted to be an architect. When he boarded the SS *Irpinia* on 18 March 1960, bound for England with his brother Erdrin, his neat, black leather bag with its protractors, T-squares, steel rulers and compasses sailed with him.

Many people from Biabou were amongst the 400 Vincentians who had paid the equivalent of £65 and boarded the boat that day. The crush was so great one young man lost his passport and papers in the deep water of the dock, and my father himself received a blow in his chest from the staff of an impatient police officer trying to hold the crowd back. My father vowed that when he made it back to Saint Vincent, he would search that officer out and give him some licks. But it was five, long, cold European winters before he could make that journey, and when he did, the policeman had long gone, redeployed to other duties or more likely creating a new life in England or the US himself.

Eight days and nights passed at sea before the passengers saw land again, the island of Madeira, where the *Irpinia* stopped to take on water. But somehow those on board still managed to find ways to have a good time, and the human souls eventually disembarking at Newquay in Cornwall now included some newly conceived.

Back in those days Dad's nickname was 'Neighbour': a testament to his good nature and the joviality which he carried with him all the way to England. Making friends was never a challenge for my father, nor was the task of helping others if he saw someone in need.

As my father and I cooked that day, if we looked in the direction of the stairs leading up from the kitchen, we could see a ledge on which were crammed colour photographs of grandchildren, graduations and the weddings of nieces and nephews. At the centre of the display was a special studio fortieth anniversary picture of my smiling parents dressed smartly but casually, full faced with health and happiness. My father was taller and standing slightly behind my smiling mother, but there was no sense of imbalance as they looked out together into the world and their home.

There was only one photograph of my father without her. It was black and white and was of him newly arrived in England, standing in an anonymous North London living room. He wore a light-grey suit, its faint stripes mirroring those on the wallpaper behind him, handkerchief in breast pocket, his right hand resting on the black briefcase which now perched on the mantel of the fireplace. I used to play with that small case of shiny instruments and tools, whose precise use I never understood, which he had protectively carried over the ocean. It had been carried all that way and then put away in cupboards in his rented rooms and our small suburban house because my father never got the chance to use those tools.

My dad's dream of designing skyscrapers, houses and public buildings did not come to pass. Instead, his first job was as a shunter on the railways, hooking together and separating carriages in Kentish Town in the cold in North London or shovelling the coal which would heat the carriages, his technical training in the Caribbean put behind him. But even through these trials, what he held on to was the memory of how he grew stronger in mind and body, and he would always laugh with amazement to see me put on gloves no matter how I protested that the conditions outside were freezing.

But he was still a creator. He and my mother made a home for our family. First, they rented rooms in a street in Dalston, and they used a small, red, rectangular tin with labelled coin slots (RENT, COAL, GAS, ELECTRICITY) to save for future plans. After my birth and when the possibility of new jobs in Luton arose, they made the short journey with me up the also infant M1 motorway and bought, wallpapered and painted the first home they owned, a house with a garden at the front and at the back. On the production lines, my father put together vehicles for Vauxhall, the originally British firm which had long been swallowed up by the American giant General Motors. The printed lettering on the tin was carefully etched over and altered: COAL became RATES, and GAS became CAR. A fifth category was added – MISCELLANY.

They planted the back garden with rose bushes at the end nearest the house, and dug and hoed to plant cabbages, lettuce, potatoes and carrots at the far end, which had a fence laced with white bells of honeysuckle. As a small child, I imagined giants bounding across the fields beyond to come and seize us up. My parents forked the clods of dark Bedfordshire earth and threw out the chunks of Chiltern chalk which I lined up as battalions of faithful soldiers to play with.

My mother and father ensured a good education for their children too, supporting us through curricula and examinations they were unused to and whose jargon they sometimes did not understand. But the importance of those studies they always recognised and accepted in the same way that they understood and supported our new activities and pastimes, like me taking care of the school rats and guinea pigs in the holidays or playing hockey instead of cricket.

When my mother and father had finally saved enough and were planning for their retirement, they built a house in Saint Vincent back in the village where my dad had been born and raised. But the Vincentians returning from England after leaving the island several decades ago now built their new homes with two or more floors and used not wood or even bricks but cement breeze blocks.

My father designed an ornate balcony on the upper floor, and he set out his areas upstairs and downstairs, inside and out, where he would spend time with family and friends. He made sure there was air-conditioning and mosquito nets aplenty for the much-anticipated visitors and relatives from overseas and that there was more than one bathroom, which would have been a luxury in England. My parents were not rich, but in Saint Vincent they had abundant access to land and the resources of the earth.

In Yorkshire in 1902, Joseph Rowntree had laid down the financial and physical foundations for the model garden village of New Earswick and stipulated that each new house should have around it a garden with fruit trees and enough ground to grow vegetables. Rowntree would have been pleased with my father's two banana trees and his kitchen garden for which the dark-green, feathery leaves of neighbouring breadfruit trees still gave shade. Dad arranged for his own breadfruit tree – which had occupied the corner of his parcel of land where his vegetable garden now was – to be moved to the local school so there was more room for the house. But he made sure he had a charcoal grill bought and ready for the dimpled, green spheres the size of bowling balls, which people regularly brought to him to be roasted. There was nothing he and my mother omitted to think of for the edifice in which he finally achieved his dream of leaving his mark on the world.

One evening after my father had gone to bed – Vincentian days began at or before sunrise and started winding down when the sun plummeted beneath the sea at around six o'clock – I found in a drawer a different list of ingredients: the inventory of goods bought to erect the house. I knew that the geological and human history of the island was dominated by the island's highest peak, the volcano La Soufrière. My parents had built their home in a land under which the lava heaved and bubbled to the extent that now scientists were trying to capture the heat and energy from the subterranean depths in the north of the island. When I uncovered that bill of goods, I discovered that in the same way that the lava flows cleared the mountain's slopes for new growth, the foundations of my parents' Vincentian house had emerged from the heat of the volcano. Each line of the list brought to my mind a response like those set out for the congregation in the Methodist prayerbooks on my parents' living room cabinet.

CONCRETE BLOCKS, SACKS OF CEMENT AND LOADS OF BOULDERS
Ejected through eruption

RABACCA MATERIAL
Harvested from the Dry River whose course was carved out by lava

SAND AND GRAVEL FROM SANDY BAY
Where still Caribs live under the shadow and threat of the Great Mountain La Soufrière

POLYETHENE
To wrap around and keep shiny furnishings unscratched

AND WIRE
Laced throughout the walls

STEEL RODS
To thread through and hold, strength fractioned in inches

ASPHALT SHINGLE and BITUMEN FELT
For the roof over our heads

ALUMINIUM WINDOWS and PANELLED DOORS
*For the passage of air to refresh us in the heat of the
Caribbean day*

SASHES
To keep the mosquitos out

LOCKS, HINGES and SCREWS
Etcetera-ed

CUPBOARDS and CLOSETS
*To hold cutlery, crockery and commemorative teacups from
our home in Luton, the Queen on some, and on others
Charles protecting Diana, or so we believed*

VINYL and CERAMIC TILES
For the bathrooms whose bidet might cause curiosity

TOILETS, WASHBASINS and BATHTUBS
To wash away our dripping sweat

ADHESIVE
*To hold all together although the invisible glue of our love
is stronger and even more permanent*

And, of course, CONTINGENCIES because Vincentians
never knew what could come next, whether hurricane, earth-

quake or fire. The last item was LABOUR. General now, paid for with honest wages and given freely. Now the descendants of slaves could build for themselves and for their families.

I had never thought that I was a maker like my father. I was not good at lighting the coals in our family fireplace, and I struggled to keep the wallpaper strips laid flat when my dad needed to spread the thick glops of glue over them or to hang them straight and unwrinkled. I thought that my cleverness lay in the retention of facts, equations and geographical locations. I was not a maker until I had a home of my own and then I dug the garden and put up the shelves; I carefully laid the blue border of dancing animals around the room above the architrave for my soon-to-be-born son. And when he was old enough to climb, I built him a treehouse because I loved him and he asked me to.

When our cooking was done, and we left the two pots to marinade their contents, I washed up all the other bowls and containers. Then we sat at the kitchen table, just the two of us, under the print of the poem 'Idyll', the windows open so that we could hear the sounds of people passing in the street outside. Our plates were laid out on the white plastic tablecloth with its pattern of yellow flowers.

When Dad indicated to me that the food's time was done, I first spooned out the thick starchy mixture onto our plates, but much more to my taste was the crimson-tinted, shrimp-laden bhaji whose liquor floated around the fungee. I wasn't sure that we had got everything right, but it tasted so nice, and we were proud.

We had made too much, and it was certain after we had given some to friends that the leftovers would stay in the fridge for a few days before we had to give them to the dogs as always. But that did not matter. We had cooked and created today, and as my dad ate, he smacked his lips, winked at me and said 'Ahhh' and that was all the 'well done' that I needed.

Lunch over, I gave my dad a last shot of Famous Grouse to take up to his recliner on the balcony for the afternoon, and then I took some time for myself to wander the broken roads threading through the village with houses rising up the hills on every side.

Because it was a national holiday, everywhere felt much quieter. Many people had left for beaches or gone on excursions or, as I had once, set off to board the ferry which travelled down the Grenadines. It had rained heavily like it did every morning, the huge, black clouds loping in from over the mountains and sliding down the coast. The downpour stopped after about ten minutes and then all around was intensely hot again.

As I walked, I wondered what else I could say that I had made, that I had created. I felt like an old brown envelope with stamps of exotic plants and birds stuck on the outside but holding inside secrets and messages which even I struggled to decipher.

The nation held on to its cultural heritage with a fierce pride, and that day all across the island celebrations were taking place to mark Independence Day. Even I was wearing a faded but precious Vincy Heat football top, given to me by my mother's friend Barbara.

When I came up the hill to the adult education centre, there seemed to be a trickle of people entering, and I followed them. A little cultural and crafts fair had been set up in the hall. *Hairouna... Land of the Blessed* read the words on the large banner which had been strung up outside, highlighting the name held for the island by its indigenous people before the arrival of Europeans and colonisation.

Inside were older ladies and young girls dressed in the yellow, green and blue national colours. Older men wore kaftan-style shirts which merged those colours with patterns and motifs of African origin. On the tables running around three walls of the halls, mementoes of Saint Vincent of yesteryear were on display: toys and photographs, and more functional items like mangles and oil-wick lanterns. I bet myself that people in the hall might assume I knew little of such things. But I could remember chats long ago with my grandmother in a room lit by lamps just like these while we drank tea whitened with condensed milk. And the months spent sleeping under her bed in a house sunk down on its knees, listening in the dark to my little red radio.

Food was on sale, the white tablecloths covered by plates filled with treats like white, glistening sugarcake islands embedded with golden peanuts and pyramids of soft brown blocks of fudge. On the floor, hemp sacks swelled with green coconuts still in their husks waiting to be chopped for the water inside. There were bulging bags of unshelled groundnuts and bags of farine ground from cassava root. The sweets on offer – such as the pastries filled with sweet, pink-coloured coconut that I now rediscovered – made me remember simple pleasures from my childhood, like being bought cheese and crackers as a treat or going to find my Uncle Percy baking bread in the shell of an oil drum in the open air.

There were drinks too: ginger beer, punch-de-crème and lemonade, and smooth strips of mauby bark with jagged ends were stacked next to jugs of the refreshing, bittersweet, mauve juice that was made when they were boiled in spiced water.

Someone had made tri-tri cakes, the delicacy which the cycle of nature gave to Vincentians and the diaspora around the world who craved them too. The fish within the cakes were literally small fry, caught during their passage back up the rivers, down which the parent adults had previously descended to lay their eggs in the sea and then die, never to return to the mountains. The tiny, translucent returning offspring were gathered and scooped up by children, women and men from river mouths where fresh water met the salt of the incoming sea. Their whole bodies were seasoned and mixed with flour, onion and grated peppers and then fried. The sharing and eating of them was part of a centuries-old human ritual as well as a migratory one. I thought that perhaps we all were like the tiny fish, trying to swim upstream to reclaim our destiny but constantly having to avoid being ensnared by the clinging nets of maturity.

I moved around the exhibits, met old friends and made new ones, several complimenting me on finding something in national colours to wear. Browsing for a souvenir to buy amongst the food, embroidered doilies and bangles, I found a set of cloth coasters in green, yellow and blue which I tucked away to bring back to England. I had thought that the place my parents called home – the dot in the ocean and on the maps of our family encyclopaedia – was just one more small island amongst many small islands. But now I knew it was far more than that – Saint Vincent was a fertile, verdant centre of Caribbean civilisation and resistance. Hairouna – Yurumein – Saint Vincent: through all the names and ages of this blessed land, the island had been a pulsing heart whose life blood had pumped all the way around the world and then found its way back to the source.

At the rear of the hall, in front of speakers and a microphone, adults filed up to make speeches whilst between those, children performed exuberant dances. Then, as the end of the afternoon came, sheets were handed out for us to sing a song.

I thought back on the meal that I had travelled 4,000 miles to make that day with my father, and the things that had come into the world because of my own endeavour and initiative. This was a song that I could sing lustily too because today, despite all the trepidation of my younger years, I now acknowledged that I could play a part in creating something worthwhile too.

Oh, there's a lovely island in the Caribbean Sea
With cocoa, citrus, coconut and fine banana trees,
There's arrowroot and sugarcane a-waving in the breeze;
Saint Vincent is its name.

REFRAIN

We're out to build a new Saint Vincent
We're out to build a new Saint Vincent
We're out to build a new Saint Vincent
The future's in our hands

We Make Mistakes All the Time

'Never Dis Di Man' played from the ghetto blaster perched on a stool outside the shop next door while men sat around a rickety table, its laminate top peeling but flat enough, and rocked back on their chairs, slapping down their faded, wooden dominoes. Sanchez's voice rang up and down the lane leading up to the heights of the village in the hills curving around the bay, his words resonating on this day of the year more than any other, *'There are lots of signs in life, Some that you may not like, You could be living this minute, The next minute you're gone away.'*

As the reggae boomed, I tried to light the candles my father and I had carried through to the rear of the carport. A nameless wind crept around the back of the house and slithered in through the vents in the breeze blocks, snuffing out all my attempts until I placed the three candles into jars to give them respite. One for each of those departed.

My dad looked on, uncharacteristically quiet, leaning on his walking stick while the two dogs snuffled around his feet. His free hand held a glass full of a liberal shot of Famous Grouse, and when I had finished, he picked up the bottle from where it sat on the plastic table and, after taking the cap off, flicked loud splashes onto the concrete near the flickering wicks.

'*Dominum nobiscum*,' he said, smiling. 'Blessings to the dearly departed.'

This habit irritated me intensely – not the homage but the waste – especially when the whisky had, at his insistence, been carted across thousands of miles from the duty-free shop at Heathrow. But for my dad, honouring the dead was more important than my disapproving stare. Even I on that last day of October 2018 felt that the spirits might be close enough to take their sip.

We heard a 'hey' behind us and, turning, I saw my uncle Fitzroy standing outside the black iron gates which guarded the vertiginous ramp up to the carport from the road. Uncle Fitzroy and his family cared for my parents with devotion when they were on the island, and the dogs did not bark or react madly in the way they did when a Rasta wheeled past with a cart full of coconuts or bananas on his head. They were as bravely fierce when one of the skinny village curs slunk past, staring back deadpan and curious at these yapping, pampered house dogs who seemed to have no idea of the licks they would get if they managed to get over the wall to fight with the local ruffnecks.

Fitzroy was in his wellington boots, and his mountain clothes were stained with dark brown earth, cutlass and hoe slung over his shoulder. He always spoke sparingly and only added to the 'hey' with a quiet 'yuh ready?'

I was. My father's age and weakness down one side of his body meant that he was now too unsteady on his feet to come

with us, but he said he would look out to try to see us when
we reached the hilltop cemetery which hung above the village.

'We coming back,' said Fitzroy, the usual Vincentian way of
saying goodbye.

We left my father nursing his drink at the table as the candles
flickered shadows across him and the dogs, who now lay on
their sides at his feet.

Fitzroy and I walked without saying anything to each other
but were very much in step as we headed back down to the main
junction of the village. We passed the empty low buildings of
the school with their slatted windows, and then the two-storey
block which housed a grocery shop and the office of the local
parliamentary representative, the red paint of the murals daubed
on the walls making political allegiance clear.

The men on the stools outside a bar barely noticed us as we
passed – they did not seem to notice each other even though,
or maybe because, they sat together every single day. Across the
road where a bridge crossed the river before it ran out to sea,
white egrets danced in the banana trees and palm fronds. The
swoosh of unseen waves grew closer. Wherever I went in Saint
Vincent, the sea was never far away.

We climbed the road in front of the open door of the
light-blue police station. In the semi-darkness behind the open
doorway, a sergeant sat behind a counter impassively, his eyes
tracking our passage across his frame of vision. At the top of
the hill, we had to cross the road by the tin-roofed bus stand.
Why this particular spot had a bus stop, and one with a roof at

that, I never understood because elsewhere it seemed that you simply had to try to flag down the careering minibuses blasting out soca and dancehall any way you could and find a way to grab their attention before they left you in their dust.

Opposite the bus stop was the football pitch, which we had to cross to reach the cemetery. When we were on the road, it had seemed that only my uncle and I had anywhere to go. But now as we walked over the uneven and tufted grass, marked out in regulation white lines, I could see groups of people and individuals heading in the same direction as us. Sometimes whole families: the adults similarly silent, determined and burdened with implements, the children with them skipping around the grassy expanse and climbing onto the huge rusty roller parked at the side of the pitch.

It was All Hallows Eve, and by tradition, every family in the village would venture out to tend and light up the graves of those they had lost. In the last days of October, children were already lighting kerosene in bamboo cannons at night to create traditional noisy 'Ba hoo!' explosions in the run-up to Guy Fawkes. Tonight though, the atmosphere was sombre and reflective, and candles and lanterns twinkled in cemeteries across the island.

We weaved our way through the tombstones, and the sound of the sea became a roar. We could almost feel the thuds of the waves as they battered the beach at the bottom of the cliff marking the limit of where the dead could be laid to rest, or in some circumstances where they were brought up from. In the fading light, the Atlantic was grey and turbulent. This was where the winds that were generated in the belly of the ocean came to. On this coast, the wildness of nature was not easily tamed and refused to quieten. Biabou was a settlement which had been whipped into existence by wind, the sea and rebellion.

When I turned and looked back, I could see the houses hugging the foothills of the mountains which stepped their way to the cloud-drenched rainforest interior. The view was beautiful – I could still pick out the yellow of the tin roof of my father's house and the pastels of newer concrete houses mixed with the wooden huts of the original Biabou villages. Biabou was changing as both money and people came back from their toil abroad, time served working in England and the US or aboard cruise ships. I could also see all the places of worship – there were eight churches in this community – which, although sprawling, held just a few hundred people. My mother's friend Barbara had joked with me that the reason there were so many churches in Biabou was because the people were so wicked.

I had no problem with the residents of Biabou, and the relatives I met greeted me with only love and encouragement. I could see though that in Saint Vincent there was also a dark seam to how people dealt with each other, which persisted in the shadows despite the drench of sunlight. Reports of sexual and domestic abuse and violence against women and children were frequent in this fervently Christian nation, and minor disputes between men could sometimes result in someone getting 'chopped' with a cutlass. Guns had found their way onto the island, and even though small growers were still able to cultivate their marijuana plots in the mountain heights far away from prying police eyes, Saint Vincent was also squarely in the sights of more organised, cross-border drug traffickers. I found Vincentians to be kind, gentle and funny but also capricious, stern – unforgiving even. Sometimes all of these within the same day.

All around us, groups of relatives bent and kneeled, scraping away the thorns and weeds which thrived more than grass in the sea air. Not far from the entrance to the graveyard, my uncle and I stopped in front of the white, earth-stained headstone of my father's mother, Esther. Near her grave lay that of her son, my Uncle Cluston, and a related cousin called Compay who I remembered very well. My father and Fitzroy were half-brothers, and the grave of Fitzroy's mother and my grandfather were a small distance away, closer to the sea. I wondered if he would leave me to go over there, but the bond between the (at least) fifteen brothers and half-brothers who my grandfather had sired was strong, and there was no divide between the two maternal lines. Tonight, we were here for the whole Rogers and Keir clan, and Fitzroy had already begun swishing at the vines that were trying to overtake the graves. I knelt and began tugging at the deep-rooted, intruding weeds with my bare hands.

I was seven years old when I met my Uncle Cluston on my very first trip to Saint Vincent with my father. I remembered him driving a jeep, with me and his wife Lucy as passengers, along clifftop roads perched above rocks and black sand beaches, which on the windward coast were buffeted by wild seas. Lucy had on a trendy, blue 1970s mod hat which stuck in my memory, and I wore a T-shirt which had 'Sand In My Shoes' embroidered beneath a smiling boy standing on a shore in his sandals. I loved that T-shirt and my expanded family, and I was as happy as a boy could be. My joy during that car ride made them smile too.

Years later, I visited my uncle again; he was now a superintendent based at the Central Police Station in Kingstown. His short-sleeved shirt shone dazzling white under the blazing Vincentian sun, a contrast to the starched and stuffy khaki he had worn when he visited us in the UK to attend a training course. I sat waiting patiently for him in his office while he dealt with business, and I watched through a different open door as a handcuffed man sat crying noiselessly in a room, awaiting his time to be questioned – suffering in plain sight.

Cluston had passed away earlier that year, quietly in a bed in his home in Mesopotamia. He was many things to many people but to me simply my favourite uncle and hero. Kindness, strength and 'family' merged in his solid human frame. When he lay silent and immobile before passing away, I wanted to call him and whisper into his silent consciousness. I wanted to tell him how I loved him and about all the places I had been to since he first filled my mind like a legendary giant.

The way I thought of Cluston was the complete opposite to how I remembered another man who family and casual acquaintances alike knew as Compay.

Compay was a headteacher and church leader, revered and respected on the island. He was also the reason it had taken me twenty years to return because behind closed doors he was addicted to alcohol and violent. He avoided, for the most part, inflicting his cruelties on his own children, but when my father in faraway England sent my sister, brother and I to stay with him, Compay found in us ready targets for his crazed rages.

Back in the UK, people of Caribbean heritage made jokes about how stern the physical punishments their parents had dealt out could be. But the occasional slipper or belt paled in comparison to the thick, heavy, cracked and faded leather straps that I saw used on pupils at school in Saint Vincent. The principal at my school – Compay – would lock all the doors bar one at a minute after nine o'clock and stand by that remaining entrance waiting to slap the strap down with all his force onto the backs or thighs of all latecomers as they ran to get in. Of course, despite the widespread acceptance of corporal punishment, most children lived in loving and supportive homes. But at the end of the day – when Compay and I left the school building – the strap came home with us.

I often wondered what would have happened if I had met Compay again alive when I was an adult. It was the one time I imagined myself deliberately hurting someone. A local saying would rise in my head: 'Me ah lightnin' and me ah ready to strike!', telling me that I was a Vincentian to my core too. But I did not get an opportunity for revenge; after we were whisked away from his care, his wife took their children and left him, and Compay drank himself into increasing stupors until he died alone and broken.

As I struggled with my childhood memories, I used to get angry with the younger versions of my parents who had sent us to Compay. One night I sat with my dad on his porch whilst rain lashed the village, and I asked him why they had entrusted our care to such a monster. Except I did not call Compay that when I spoke to my dad; I knew he still respected and felt connected to this man who we were related to, and my father did not know all of the punishments that had fallen upon us.

'We were just trying to do the best for we as a family,' was what he whispered to me in the truest and most honest way. And I realised that through all their travels, my mother and father had also been damaged by the pain of the choices they had to make.

Winston, Cluston, Compay. Joined by blood and by their life journey to relative success from humble beginnings.

Another of my father's half-brothers, Selwyn, had also made the journey to settle in England – in his case to Reading rather than Luton or High Wycombe – and then had returned to the Caribbean many years before my dad to rejoin the children he left behind. His family were not as well off as they might have been if Uncle Sel had stayed on in the UK, but they were happy. I would visit and sit down with him because I loved him, and Uncle Selwyn would quote to me from religious texts and reassure me that the Lord knew best.

As I pulled myself upright from tending Compay's resting place, I looked down at my hand and saw that the soil of my abuser's grave was still deep under my fingernails. 'We hafi satisfy,' Selwyn had told me innumerable times, and I remembered that as Fitzroy and I gathered our tools and walked back down the hill.

Catherine and Richardson

1813, Newington

Richardson's house was perched at the start of a terrace of other narrow cottages off a bend of the road that led to the Horsemonger Lane Gaol. He kept a small garden at the front in which he planted bulbs and cuttings during the months he was not travelling, for the reward of the colours that greeted him when he did return here.

From the garden, he stepped straight into the small room that he used as his parlour, tidy and precisely ordered to make best use of the limited space. Behind the parlour was his kitchen, and above, the room where he slept. On the top storey was a room stacked with the paraphernalia of thirty years of being 'The Penny Showman', crisscrossing the countryside and towns with his entourage. Dusty panoramas leant against the walls, and stacks of playbills filled the floor. Sometimes, slowly, he would climb the stairs to that third floor and with a lantern sit and remember the wonders of nature he had exhibited to the world.

Tonight, as always, Richardson was alone at home. He slumped back in his beaten old armchair as the bells of Southwark Cathedral chimed one short of the dozen. He had not yet bothered to take off his boots and hat or his old black coat, to which dust still clung from the tramps he took round the streets and squares to find places suitable for putting on his dramas and performances.

The popularity of the fairs was declining. The previously enthusiastic burghers, whose acceptance and permissions to pitch he had relied on, were now increasingly inclined to protest that his players and exhibitions offended the tastes of their townspeople: the same customers who had previously brayed with delight at all the exotic curiosities of the travelling theatre. Still the show ploughed on across the southern counties from Southampton to Basingstoke, Marlow, Saint Albans and now London. He still preferred wherever he could to sleep in his caravan, but he had put down roots too here in South London, a place where he could go to church each Sunday to worship and, when the time came, to baptise a child.

The chatter and shouts of drunks staggering and jostling their way home from the inn were beginning to die away, but as his eyelids began to droop, a knock startled and woke him.

'Who the hell is it?' he shouted at the closed door.

'You have a visitor, Mr Richardson sir.'

'A visitor? What fecking visitor at this hour of night?'

Even as he spoke, Richardson strode to the door, unlocked and pushed it open, so hard that the person standing on the other side had to jump backwards.

What Richardson first saw was one of the local boys standing outside with a lantern in his hand. Behind him was a woman – at first Richardson could tell this only by the outline of her bonnet – her silhouette dimmed in the darkness of the street although the lights of the city itself shimmered above the rooftops.

The boy was very young, and nervousness quickened his words.

'She said she's come to see you, sir. She was knocking at all the doors, and me mam said to bring her to you. She said she's got a letter.'

He thrust out a much folded and handled piece of paper which nonetheless had the rich thickness of vellum and bore ornate lines of fine handwriting.

'Feck off with that nonsense,' Richardson said, waving the letter away. 'I cannot read that, woman! Come in and tell me what it says! And, boy – you can feck off too!'

The lad did not need much prompting and, pushing the letter back into the woman's hand, he scurried into the darkness.

The bustle and strangeness of London had overwhelmed Catherine, and she was glad to find quiet in this sheltered road. She stepped just within the doorway, bending her head to pass beneath its frame. She looked down at the short, elderly white gentleman who had invited her in and wondered how someone who held the power and wealth she had heard about could be dressed so badly. The wool of his black coat was tufted and bobbled, and the brass buttons of the red waistcoat beneath it were too tarnished to shine. His corduroy breeches bulged at his thighs over thick, worsted stockings, which, like his shoes, were dappled with the mud thrown up by four days of the fair back up at Smithfields, which she had visited first to make her enquiries.

'What's that you hold, woman?'

'Sir, it a letter from mi mistress. It say wha' mi come here fah.'

'And what is that? For money I wager? Careful what you say now. There's a gaol full of swindlers up the road, and among them are some others who thought they could fool me!'

'No, sir. For mi son, sir. For mi boy. Where he be, sir?' she asked, 'Is here he be nah? Wit' yuh nah tru?'

And then Richardson looked properly at her and saw it in her eyes. He saw in her face and in the bow of her neck an echo of George. His George.

He stammered and mumbled as he answered. 'The boy is gone now.'

'Gone, sir? Yuh mean him sell again. Oh Lawd, sir, where mi hafi go now…!'

'No, no… I don't mean he has left. I mean he is dead. Eighteen months now.'

She did not fall to her knees or wail. She did not bend her head back and let a keening scream escape from deep within the way her mammy did when her daddy fell while he dug out arrowroot and never got up again. She simply stood there, thin and imposingly tall, head nearly touching the roof of the small room, all the rage in her eaten away after months of travelling and grieving. All that happened was that her face twitched and moved as she struggled to absorb the finality of what she had heard, her head spinning at the pronouncement that ended her search – a search she had known was doomed anyway but which had been the only reason she had to keep going.

'Where is he now, sir? Where is mi boy?'

'He's in Marlow. I gave him a good Christian burial. A fine one. You've no need to worry about that. Sit now, young lady, before you fall.'

He pulled a chair out for her from under a small desk and sat himself back in his armchair.

'I did my best for him, I promise. Brought four of the finest doctors from the Royal College of Surgeons out here to see to him and paid for them meself. But he got worse month after month and was in such pain. And then the swelling on his jaw grew so large…'

The woman gasped, and Richardson realised he had said too much, too quickly.

'Are you alright?'

She shook her head, but still no tears came. 'Where is Marlow, sir?'

'It's about two days' travel from here. I can take you there if you want.'

'Sir, mi hafi get back to my lady and master dem. Dem ah wait for mi and will be vex if mi nah get back soon.'

She looked at the wall and amongst the small frames saw a drawing of a little naked boy. He had mainly pale-white skin across his body, but she recognised him instantly and felt her chest clench with maternal anguish. His body was speckled with spots of black, and he had black bands on either side of his face. George was sitting on a turtle with a ring in his ear and the beginning of a smile on his face, and he was reaching out to offer a leaf to a dog which had the same pattern of spots that the boy bore.

'It's alright. I will take care of that. I have money. Plenty of it. And need of a help round here. The people with me now are wastrels *and vagabonds with a fear of hard work. If you have made it this far, I doubt the same applies to you. What is your name?'*

'Catherine, sir.'

'Well, Catherine, come. I will show you where your boy is buried. I want to put up my headstone. I want you to see that it is done and to make sure it is next to his. I took care of him for you. So let me have that please.'

There was a crackle in his voice, and he kept his weathered top hat and his eyes lowered as they sat, the only movement coming from the shadows as a lamp flickered.

Finally, Catherine nodded, and the tears began to stream down her face. Richardson reached his arm out to put a hand on her shoulder and to steady her as all the weights of the world threatened to cave her in. Outside, the wind blew north along the mile or so towards the river, where it would play with the small waves that lapped against the sandy foreshore.

Part VI

COMING HOME

Home and Away

As a child in Luton, I was liked well enough and had friends from different backgrounds and cultures. Childhood worries like feeling lonely or being bullied were hardly ever a problem for me. Sometimes though it felt that the things I was passionate about were not valued. In my youth, difference in the UK Black community was not always celebrated, whether from outside or within. Sometimes that was the effect of stereotyping, and sometimes it seemed that the pain of constant rejection and discrimination meant that we felt more strength gathered behind a single shield, a collective way of being.

Often I felt that I stuck out and was the odd one for jumping on the train to go and explore galleries in London ('What do you want to go and do that for?'), strange for choosing to go to university ('Are there any Black people there?') and, later, weird for choosing to travel to Aotearoa ('Black people don't go to those kinds of places.').

In the sports I played, I also felt different from many of my peers. Although I played a little football and rugby, my chosen game was hockey. Once, as a teenager, I broke a finger playing hockey just before I attended a socialist conference in London, and when a stern, left-wing lady saw my injured hand in a cast and heard my explanation, she told me off for playing the game of the oppressors. I wanted to reply that I played in a team with the sons of migrants from the Indian subcontinent; that their fathers were car workers like my dad, not businessmen from leafy shires. But I am not sure she would have heard me any more than the other people who thought there was only one way I should be, look or sound.

I wanted to feel comfortable in my skin and to be validated by all my influences and connections. To be accepted whoever I was with, even though the orange of my first-ever Luton Town top laid out on my bed thrilled me far more than the white shirts of the England team when I watched football on TV. I had to travel to shores far away in miles and memory to find out that it was alright to do things differently from those around me.

Being with the boys and men I played hockey with was another kind of homecoming. Pure happiness for me was driving back to Luton with three or four others, all of us chatting loudly the whole way. Along the A-roads, we told and retold the story of that afternoon's game, reminiscing about the sprints, tackles, shots and sometimes red cards and confrontations which were the highlights of our latest endeavour. Sometimes we would laugh about our experiences of urban Brown culture colliding with attitudes in more rural and less diverse settings as we drove out eastwards each week from Luton. We won titles and leagues in our own right, travelling to places like Boston and Bury, Maldon and Spalding – places we had only known before from an AA atlas index or heard on About Anglia or in weather reports.

We giggled for ages about arriving in an eastern county hours before a game and asking for directions from the first random stranger only to be told straight away, 'You'll be that lot from Luton for the hockey match, won't you?' Our reputation and the colour of our skins preceded us. But that could not dim our glow as we relaxed with each other and chatted rubbish on the way to our games or when we drove home in the autumn sunshine after winning 4–3 away.

Back in my parents' house in Biabou, on the cabinets and low tables and amongst the pictures of our family and cousins, nephews, nieces, weddings and anniversaries, there nestled signs of sporting glories achieved a long way away. There were my father's small darts trophies, usually the gold-plated figure of a man poised in mid-throw. But also my hockey trophies, circular medals emblazoned with crossed sticks on a green background. Hockey, the game of my youth, had travelled all the way to be with me here in the Caribbean. It had so often been a refuge for me, an anchor of familiarity and a way to meet people when I left home for university or to work in Aotearoa.

But the hockey medals brought back other, less positive memories too. Memories of reactions and anger whose origins had perhaps been seeded in the trauma of separation on Saint Vincent decades before. I remembered the boy my age who I punched at an annual six-a-side tournament – I was taller than him, but we had squared up to each other and inside I had a dread fear that he was going to hit me first, so I made sure that could not happen. I recalled too an opposition player who grunted monkey noises at me and who I chased around the hockey pitch, unable to catch him despite my longer legs because of the simple scientific advantage that fear and adrenaline gave him. That was almost cartoonishly funny, but when in another match the monkey noises came again from someone unidentified this time, I remonstrated with the opposition captain in their half-time huddle for him to control his players. But no sympathy, confession or apology came.

Throughout my teenage years and twenties, I could not trust my reactions. I would readily intervene to stop other players fighting, but if the umpire misinterpreted the situation and brandished his yellow or red card at me, I could be transformed into a human tornado of swear words and fury, other teammates having to pull or push me off the pitch. And then after the tsunami of anger came the guilt and the labels, the ones that others used to damn me, and the ones I was more than ready to stick on myself.

But I was held by family and friends and by a team of brown-skinned men who saw more in me than my anger. Men who understood that a Black man being angry did not automatically mean that I was being aggressive. They never condoned my outbursts, but they did not write me off as a thug either – they saw the man I was and the man I could become and tenderly cradled both. With these teammates, it was safe for me to be me. In that club I knew I belonged.

Our roots were in faraway places: our families were sprung from the soil of India, Pakistan, Uganda, Kenya, Sri Lanka,

South Africa and the Caribbean. Our parents, uncles and aunties had crossed wide oceans to do their bit, to make a better world, a better Empire, and were proud of all they had to offer the new country they would come to call home. They dreamt of their children becoming teachers, lawyers and engineers, architects and doctors. Dreams which through perseverance and diligence often came true, even though all our parents had to swim through a sea of challenges as their children became 'first-one-in-the-family-to'. They had to make sense of an educational and examination system which had diverged widely from the standards and rigour colonialism had imposed on the Commonwealth before the Empire retreated.

Our fathers and mothers toiled day and night, in shops and factories, driving and delivering, walking echoing warehouses to pick parts and make cars. But for the men at least there was an escape. As well as endeavour and hard work, they brought a passion for sport and skills honed on dusty fields playing with coconut-palm cricket bats and battered, plastic footballs. They took on the British Empire's old games and blew new life into them, bringing flair, speed and athletic splendour to the sedate playing fields of Home County towns and villages. Or in my dad's case to the midweek pub darts leagues of Luton.

Our fathers formed clubs of their own to join the local domestic leagues, teams where there was no judgement for them not drinking alcohol or if they slipped into their mother tongue in the changing room. They were not trying to feel separate or superior; all they wanted was to relax and enjoy themselves in this new land and to find their own way to settle into life here. Hoping that in sport, at least, there would be at last a level playing field to occupy with their workmates and neighbours: people with whom they shared the same workplaces and shopping centres, whose children attended the same schools, but whom society gave greater status to because they had been born in England, and their passports and papers did not have the caveats of registration or naturalisation.

By the 1970s, Asian and West Indian cricket clubs had become renowned sporting institutions in their respective towns. In the south of England, hockey clubs such as Slough, Ramgarhia and Indian Gymkhana, and works teams like Ford and Vauxhall, broke records and created legends. Dark-skinned men who were overlooked or insulted on weekdays gained grudging respect for their dazzling stickwork, tenacity and commitment as they blazed through the weekend. And when the Windies cricket dished out a 'blackwash' or Olympic hockey medals were won, that generation allowed themselves to express a raucous support, which implied no lack of loyalty to the land they had migrated to. They were simply demonstrating their bond with and fierce pride for internationally renowned brothers who had emerged from the same cradle which had nurtured their own humbler skills. Skills and achievements they tried to practise and display themselves, on small local grounds on cold rainy Saturdays with barely anyone to watch, but with the promise and warmth of the stories they could share in their cars on the journey home.

My teammates and I matured and grew up together. High-school kids became sixth formers and then university students and doctors, bankers, builders, managers and social workers. As our fathers retired and the factories closed, still their sons played on, even though official recognition and county or regional selection were hard to achieve.

As we grew older and our waistlines thickened, we still huffed and puffed each weekend, but now as proud parents ourselves, we would bring along our children to watch, although usually they simply ran along the sidelines playing with each other. Eventually some of the young ones would cross the white lines themselves and fill the gaps created by domestic responsibilities and weekend work shifts for their parents. Now in the team there were teachers and leaders, healers and makers, energising the hearts of our town and our workplaces. We helped where we could the communities around us and overseas, not waiting to be asked to go to the aid of those in need. Just as our parents aspired to, we achieved.

Once I tried to engage the attention of a prominent journalist who also came from Luton to ask them to write about how some of my clubmates had organised their own relief response and expedition to their families' homelands in Pakistan after devastating floods there. I wanted to reverse the usual narrative that people in those distant places could only be rescued by powerful, European-led NGOs or that the only thing which came out of Luton was trouble. I wanted to help the sharing of this untold story of a diaspora not waiting for governments to step in but organising their own response instead. That journalist and I exchanged a brief flurry of emails and then their interest died away because other priorities were thought more newsworthy.

We could shrug off the small hurts and even smile back at the stares in those rural towns, where on matchdays everyone for miles around seemed to know we were on the way. But the racism and wounds could sometimes cut deeper: just-muffled-enough taunts of 'wog' and 'Paki' on the field of play, insults which the umpires never seemed to hear or think important enough for the game to be halted. When they came the monkey noises behind our backs from opposition players were not punished, and those who made them were never brave enough to stand and do it to our faces because they knew we would not tolerate it or back away. Not all games were like this. But there were enough for us to remember that we were seen as the 'other' and as the outsiders.

The time came when we seemed to lose as often as we won and were relegated as well as promoted. We were battered in farming outposts as agricultural tackles flew in but caught each other before we fell and held out a hand when we stumbled. Despite the spite and tensions that could sometimes be there in our games, the sense that everyone was against us, we could offer that hand to opponents too. I only ever once saw a player helped off limping by two from the other side, his arms draped across their shoulders, and when it happened, it was my team-mates doing the carrying.

I once overheard a player at a previous club saying, 'He only tackles well cos he's got long arms, and he only gets out fast at short corners because he's got long legs! That's all he's got!' That was all it took to shrink my self-esteem and rob me of my confidence. From then onwards, I internalised that I was just a tall bloke with long legs and that any of my athletic achievements could only be the result of luck and genetics. Somehow that skewed attribution never seemed to happen for white players, whether amateur ones or for the footballers we watched on Saturday nights on *Match of the Day* – they were allowed to be gifted.

It took me a long time and the validation of my new team-mates to unlearn that nonsense and to take pride in what I could do. I had to be told by more supportive voices that the reason I was a good defender was because I knew how to tackle legally and cleanly without fouling people (mostly) and that I was fast because I could see situations developing and get there first. The men in this club taught me that the way of the world is that some people are going to get upset about anything you do with passion and commitment, and that might lead to flare-ups. But their discomfort or dislike of my interventions did not automatically mean that I was doing anything wrong any more than it did when I made a crunching but fair tackle on the playing field.

We took a quiet, smiling pride in each other and were all the validation that we needed. From others, the judgements which stuck were never about all we had given – to our town, our community and our sport – but instead described how we did not fit in or follow the rules. Or set out the need to bring us to heel. Despite that, my club represented for me many, many wonderful things. I realised that we were a good team because we had each other. Our skins were black and brown, our home was Luton, and our strength was in our togetherness.

Although I loved being with my teammates, after my parents had moved from Luton and with my weekend family commitments in London, the distance to travel back for games gradually became too much for me to get to see them more than once or twice a season, let alone play. I fell out of touch with the club as my life for a while also seemed to lose its anchors and security. My visits to Luton only became frequent again when my parents came back from Saint Vincent, and I accompanied and took my mother to hospital appointments. I usually drove up and stayed overnight, but sometimes I got the train from London and then my mother and I would book a cab for the next day.

On one of these midweek trips, I caught the slow stopper train up from Kentish Town after work and, disembarking in Luton, began my slow walk over the railway bridge into Hightown. It was slow because my heart was heavy, and my shoulders sagged with the weight of worries about my mother and my whole life changing. A voice had to repeat itself twice to shake my minds' attention out of its gloom.

'Alex! Alex! Hey, mate!'

It was Yas, one of those old teammates and a good friend. Yas was one of those who was usually the first to calm me down and support me when I got into an on-pitch squabble, to get between me and the player I was seeking a fight with or to usher me off the pitch. Yet afterwards in the changing room or in the bar where we drank tea and munched sandwiches, Yas and the others would talk with and look at me with the same friendship, regard and affirmation.

We exchanged the usual work-related pleasantries and then Yas asked me a question.

'How you doing, mate?'

And because we were close, I told him, and he listened silently.

'Sorry to hear that, mate. Really sorry. Hey, we're still playing, you know. All the old guys. Me and Amjid and Brajinder, Imran and Saj. We've got a match at home this Saturday. What are you up to? Fancy a game?'

'Yes,' I said, my heartbeat quickening in my chest. 'Yes I'd really, really like that.' And all of a sudden I felt not quite so alone. I felt like part of something bigger again. Part of a team.

Keep the Faith

I think so much about what I want to share about that Sunday in 2019 with someone close to me, absent but not departed. Like the oval of light at the end of a railway tunnel, I want to show what still connects us and to light up the way home. This was a world uncovered and laid bare. This is what is waiting for them to come back to. Because return is what we are always able to do.

There were only the three of us who got into the car that day: my father, Tom and me. My dad who now walked so slowly, his back bent over by the grief he bore on his shoulders. I too was hollowed out by the disappearance from my life of people I loved. Tom was so quiet – I don't think he knew what he was heading into or what he was meant to do when we got there. The clouds above Luton were grey and swirling, and their turbulence matched our mood.

That lunchtime, we were visiting Mrs Wright just like in the old days when I was young. Back then there was me, Anthony and Alison squeezed onto the back seat of the Vauxhall Victor, fighting and teasing each other through every mile of our imprisonment. On each of the roads I drove down now, my father had a memory of who had lived there and which island they had come from, or, if they were Vincentian, which small village. On the way from Hightown to Hockwell Ring, like he had on a different car ride the year before, he educated and reminded us of the community he and my mother had been part of for fifty years. Marsh Farm had always felt edgy when I used to stray there on my bicycle, other kids on the streets unsmiling as we passed each other on the aptly named Strangers Way. Now the tower blocks had been knocked down, and the estate had come through riots and stigma to become – well let's say peaceful and respectable. The migrants who arrived in the 1960s with education and aspirations had brought their ambitions, and the neighbourhood had absorbed those too.

Mrs Wright stood outside her house while I reversed into place. She was the same age as my dad, and her story was woven around his and my mother's. On the steps she kissed and hugged us all, and the months since we had last been together fell away.

'It's been so long,' she said. 'Come, come inside – it too cold out here.'

She led us into the narrow hallway of her home. As we walked down, I caught a glimpse through the living-room door of coffee tables and shelves adorned with mirrors, wedding and graduation photographs, and vases of plastic flowers, beautiful in their unpollinated splendour. Today we were not going to be sitting on the pristine front-room sofas; Mrs Wright took us straight through to the cosy dining room at the rear of the house. There the table was set like it was every Sunday to welcome those who needed rest, a meal or just company. And often more than that.

Over the years, many people had made the journey to this small house and had come to call Mrs Wright their 'aunty'.

The reason for our lunch invitation was to mark two birthdays: mine and my father's, nearly but not quite on the same day. My dad often told the story of how I had begun my journey into the world on the same date that he was born but that I had hung on until just past midnight because I could not bear to share the limelight with anyone else. This made me laugh because surely it was the other way round – I thought that perhaps he in his vanity had been a little relieved when he realised that a day for celebration remained his and his alone.

But not today. Inside, a group of ladies waited for us, as fiery and feisty as ground spice. There were five of them, heights from short to tall, but all strong and sturdy in that way Caribbean women are: Velma, Sandra, Viola, Annette and Mabel. The last was seemingly concentrating on her dancing knitting needles but managing to keep an eye on the rest of us over the glasses halfway down her nose.

Only one person was missing from the circle – my mother – and her friends wanted to honour her family. These women were all linked by bonds forged as they raised families in this Bedfordshire town far from the island which they still always called 'home'. They had met through church or work: a couple had known my mother through their decades working at the Luton and Dunstable Hospital, walking the maternity wards together in the dead of night. Thousands of babies delivered, and many bereaved parents comforted, life somehow finding a way to continue.

The table nearly filled the compact room, and to squeeze around it the women had to trundle one by one through the gap between its edge and the wall. Now they waited for my father to occupy the place at its head, Tom and I on either side. He came in behind me, standing a little straighter now but still unsteady with every step. Now his eyes had that sparkle of someone who was simply 'too troublesome' as my mum used to say, and his mouth began throwing out compliments and insults in all directions. In jokes and chat, the pensioners returned to the shores of their youth. They basked in memories of friendships begun far away and which were continued as they stitched car seats together or wandered cavernous warehouses to find obscure vehicle parts.

I realised there were two other women there, hidden away preparing food in the adjoining kitchen. The older, Lena, was my age, but I didn't know her at all from my years growing up in this town. A deep sadness in her eyes told part of her story; she seemed to bear her own weight of gratitude, and I thought that perhaps she had once been one of those lost wanderers. She and her daughter busied themselves preparing the meal, the younger woman stealing out intermittently to the garden for a fag and to text.

They began carrying in dishes and bowls, and the feast began. Rice and chicken, black-eyed peas and roast potato served onto plate after never-ending plate. Coleslaw piled on the side. There was duck swimming in juice and ripe, tender beef. Brown rice and plantain piled in a golden mound. At the start there was squash to drink and mauby and sorrel, then ginger beer or Prosecco. And when those were finished, my father still wanted more so they brought out Buck's fizz, and there was the pop of corks to celebrate us all being together. Then the real talking began. Oh, the stories we heard that day! My father loved having an audience, and his cockiness rose to meet the gentle teasing from these women who could deal with his foolishness all day long.

'Yuh, yuh like to talk so!' they took turns in reminding him, as he told tale after tale of how age meant nothing to him and how his physiotherapist was so impressed by his strength and vigour.

When I asked him if he would like his beef cut up, the reply I got was a disdainful, 'Mi nah so crampy yet!' But I just waited for a moment when he was distracted by his own laughter and then discreetly separated the succulent flesh into smaller pieces.

In their conversation, the elders sometimes uncovered things that made them suck their teeth. They spoke about the rudeness of the 'youth dem' down at the chippie, effing and jeffing and dressed like 'dem trousers nah have nuh belt and ah slip down to show dem batty'. They excluded Tom from their disapproval though, instead praising him for his politeness and the passion of a speech he had made at his school about a racist encounter, his oration watched on the tiny screen of a mobile phone which was passed around the table. There was applause around the room after the video had finished, but the women had to clap their hands towards an empty chair because Tom had left the room out of embarrassment. But he could not escape the second round of kisses and proud embraces waiting for him when he ran out of reasons to avoid the dining room or places to hide in the house.

The tiny, hibernating computer screen perched in the corner which once a week Mrs Wright used to check her emails caught my father's attention. It prompted him to share a tale about how when their first domestic TVs lost signal, he and his West Indian friends would say the fluttering, pixelated black-and-white screen was 'frosty'. He told us that he loved when the Columbia lady appeared at the start of a film with her torch and blue cape because he knew her presence meant the movie would be a great one.

The afternoon was a journey of reminiscence and whimsy, not drinking rum and playing dominoes with his male friends like back in the day but filled with warmth and companionship in the same way. And while Dad was holding forth, the mother who was cooking in the kitchen told me how she was so proud of Tom for speaking up against injustice and racism.

The elders went back too, into dark memories holding things that had scared and hurt them even though they were of a generation that did not like to dwell on the bad times. Voices grew quieter and the silences a little longer. Recollections of freezing day after shivering night, hearing 'wog' and 'sambo' casually tossed into speech by the people they worked alongside on the trains and buses, and in the canteens and wards which kept the Empire's heart beating. Maybe the old people thought they would be alright as well because of their long-held fealty to Queen and Country, and because the national anthem was sung out across the Commonwealth for royal birthdays by ranks of schoolchildren in immaculate khaki uniforms. Perhaps the expectation of instant acceptance on arrival in this cold land meant the pain of rejection was even sharper – the same pain I felt decades later when a work colleague used the phrase 'nigger in the woodpile' without embarrassment or even catching breath.

Not seeing the punch coming is what gets us all. But that Sunday the pain of remembering did not outweigh the strength gained from surviving. 'Keep the faith,' my father would always say. 'Keep the faith and carry on.'

I had never heard this before, but my father shared how he had been chased by teddy boys with knives and knuckledusters through the streets of London shortly after arriving on the *Irpinia*. He was saved only by the kindliness of a Jamaican stallholder who hid him behind canvas and pallets. Why his pursuers ignored the stallholder's Blackness he didn't know.

Velma, diminutive and plump, seemed to rise with pride as she remembered walking out on the seemingly courtly GP who told her, 'Madam, I couldn't possibly know how to treat the illnesses of Black people!' And Mrs Wright shared her astonishment at the smartly dressed African who used his umbrella without hesitation on the white woman who swore at him for wanting to take the seat next to her on a bus.

And still my dad talked and talked.

Tom and I shared a smile when he told everyone that he planned to run the London Marathon in April. After that, he said he would fly home to Saint Vincent to look after himself, and sadness rose within me. He spoke about how he would tend his kitchen garden of herbs and cook up leftovers for the spoilt dogs.

I remembered how surprised I was when I saw those dogs for the first time. I could not shake the thought that we were never allowed any pet larger than a goldfish when I was a child. Old age had allowed my parents to live the way they wanted to live too. Dad laughed remembering how his grandchildren, my sons, would attempt to ride those dogs, in between the hours they spent trying to coax out the fat crapo which lived in the drainage channel.

He described how once he got back 'he, one, himself' would chop coconut husks with a cutlass and roast breadfruit over them till the skin was black and the flesh inside was moist and soft. In truth, I knew it would be one of the boys in the village who he would give five dollars to come tend the breadfruit, but for my dad to always be in charge was fine and just as things should be.

The words swam and darted like small fish in the sea, circling and flowing until they bolted away as my father collapsed in grief when his mind went back to a night two months before. That was when my mother had slipped away from us. His right hand covered his heart in the Vincentian salute to someone who could not be there. And then he held my hand and told me that the September afternoon when he and my mother left me at a provincial hall of residence was the hardest day of his life. I was left speechless at this confession; I had never imagined him missing me so much. Truly, fathers love in ways that sons never know.

The time came for us to get back in our car and drive away, but something was different from when we had arrived. We had found devotion we had forgotten was there for all of us. My dad yawned and stretched his arms above his head and said how he would sleep so well that night, partly because of the food and wine but mostly due to the whole nutmeg in its mace jacket that he always carried in his pyjama breast pocket.

Mabel sized him up carefully, and the clicking of the needles stopped. She told him the reason he slept so well and so often wasn't because of any of that nonsense but because he was so worn out and old now.

My father returned her stare flatly and allowed a perfect pause before he said loudly 'I'm not old. I'm senior!'

And with that he stood up, waggled his hips, did a little dance on the spot and the room erupted in a wave of warm laughter sweeping us home.

My Girlfriend Cuts My Hair

The first time that my girlfriend cut my hair she turned the trimmer this way and that, despite my protestations that it should be held flat against my skull for maximum extraction and to let the blades see some action. I perched on the rim of the bath next to the shower cubicle and looked up as she circled me, held in her orbit by love. Blonde tresses tumbled down over her shoulders, and her lips were pursed in concentration and nervousness that she might graze me or miss a bit.

But the next time that my girlfriend cut my hair, she radiated confidence and intent. The trimmer whirred like a fine motorcar as she guided it this way and that – now she possessed a barber's mojo of her own. Sometimes it might disappear for a while, but it always came back.

As she tended my hair, tiny whorls, surprising in their volume, tumbled between my back and the fabric of my dressing gown, and tightly wound loops fell on the lino between my feet, herding together in supportive flocks on the black-and-white squares.

My girlfriend cut my hair again, the strokes of the trimmer caressing my head in slow, gentle revolutions. I hated how my hair now grew in incoherent patches, but somehow she found a way to make what remained look neat and even. She cut my hair, and I closed my eyes and drifted in a sea of dozing remembrance.

Before my girlfriend began to cut my hair, the only person close to me who wanted, or was allowed, to touch it was my father, who used stern authority to keep me pinned onto a kitchen chair. Who else could cut our hair except people we let down all our defences for? Only those who care about how we go out into the world are granted permission to get near to the highest and most exposed part of ourselves. Only those we trust intimately are allowed to touch the crowns of our glory.

Once a month he did this, year after year, and each time I endured the ritual teasing at school about the severity of my shearing. I think that at those times the catcalls of 'Bean-heaaaaad!' in the playground were particularly shrieking.

Then one day as a teenager I went to town with money in my pocket, to visit a hairdresser's shop full of Caribbean accents and chat, and my father never cut my hair again. Eventually I moved away to university, not knowing or caring what barbers would be there, and I found ways to shape my 'fro which I had not dared try in Luton.

Those shops were full of rapid speech about football and cricket, and R&B pumped out of huge, wall-mounted screens. At first, I felt shy and out of place amongst the noise, but gradually I understood that it was alright to stay quiet and I could sit comfortably enjoying the cacophony, even slipping into sleep.

But when my girlfriend and I found each other and she began cutting my hair, we had our own private banter – 'You're my YTS and I'm teaching you customer service,' I told her, and she in turn threatened to leave me half-bald or asked when I intended to start paying. But at the end we looked into her bathroom mirror together with no arguments or unhappiness. We simply caught the reflection of each other's gaze and without speaking thought… *Well done.*

As he grew old, I began cutting my father's hair, just like he used to trim mine until I thought myself too big to sit on the chair in the kitchen and have my hair cut by my dad. I cut his in the front room of a Hightown terrace whose light came from the rays of weak afternoon sunshine pushing through the small windows and net curtains. This was where my mother and father had come back to live when her weight dropped drastically and the doctors in Saint Vincent ran out of the knowledge and equipment to diagnose what was happening. My parents had spent more time in the Caribbean in their retirement, but their attachment to this country and their family in England was so strong that they always found a reason to come back to the UK once the bitter (as they felt it) English winter was over.

But this return to Luton was filled by scans and assessments. They stayed in a house owned by my brother, and my mother would sit and read *The Mirror* or do the crossword while I used the recliner next to hers as my barber's chair.

My father's tufts were now as sparse as mine, although I kept mine deliberately so in a middle-aged man's way, erasing all in order to hide absence. Grey growth still exploded behind my father's earlobes, as astonished as a time traveller finding themselves materialised alone on a sterile future landscape. But still he asked me to cut and preen and remove the bristles inside his nose and ears so that he could remain the dandy he had always been. He always wanted to look his best if friends were coming to take him for a pint of Guinness at the Irish pub on the corner, though the passage of years meant that his group of buddies was much smaller now.

When they passed away, they left rich memories and stories – tears of laughter came back to my eyes remembering my father and his friend in Tottenham cursing the liberal amounts of 'perma-straight' pomade they had slapped on before nights out in London in the 1960s. They blamed it for making them 'shit like ducks' and definitely, absolutely, undeniably, being the cause of their hair falling out in later years.

In the months while my mother's illness was investigated, I sat many times in the barbershop of a terse but kind Nigerian back in Hightown, seizing opportunities for a quick cut before jumping on the train back to London and the flat where I lived alone. This was after my mother and I had waited quietly on hard clinic chairs for her ten minutes with the smartly dressed consultant whose striking tie always distracted me. Her decades of service in this very same hospital were not a detail worth noting in the Manila file which he held but barely looked at.

A nurse would hover nearby or perch on the bed, ready to mop up the impact of his words, giving them meaning in the same way that I opened and translated the piles of white envelopes from social services, Macmillan or Age Concern. I tried to hack a path through the briars of tangled agencies surrounding my mother who, after years of caring for my father, was now the service user.

From the window at the front of the Nigerian's shop, the barber could see the elderly Black lady bustling every day with her shopping bags up and down the road that led to the town centre. As he cut my hair and talked to me about Arsenal and what a lovely woman my mother was, we both looked out on the church where just a few months later the hymns would ring out for her funeral service.

My mother went back to Saint Vincent one last time before the round of treatment which we were sure would allow her an ending she and we were in control of. It would give her one more Christmas, one more summer, one more chance to give her grandchildren treats for their birthdays.

My brother and I took our parents back home to the grand house they had built with remittances earnt unstintingly over decades working on hospital wards and in draughty factory halls. The table in the corner of their carport was filled with bananas, guava, mangoes, golden apples and breadfruit as family and friends came to say goodbye. Her adventure, which began sixty years before on a dock in Kingstown, small suitcase at her feet, was coming to an end in the bosom of her island again.

Sometimes the stream of visitors and their tendency to companionably linger in that Vincentian way was tiring for her, and she would retreat to lie down in the bedroom. Anger could quickly rise in her at how intensely people spent time doing nothing, and she would get stressed and impatient – cancer tries to steal not only cells but also spirit and the semblance of the person we all thought we knew. But she would always smile and call back to the people shouting her name as they passed down the road in front of the house, and she knew the names of all the little children who politely said good afternoon as they skipped past the gates.

I escaped to the local karaoke bar one Saturday evening, and coming back late to find whisky, I expected to be shouted at like a teenager when she discovered me rattling through the cupboard bottles. But my mother treated me like I was coming home from school, and in the middle of the night we shared a cup of tea and a chat like we always used to in the kitchen where my dad had cut my hair.

I only remember my mother telling one out-and-out joke, and she shared it on that last trip to her birthplace.

We drove to the north of the island one day, our journey washed in perpetual sunshine, she and I on the back seat, and the little jeep struggled as it tried to climb the hills bordering the parish where she had started her career as a teacher. As I heard the engine over-revving and threatening to die before it reached the top of the next ascent, I asked, 'Mum, how do they do MOTs in Saint Vincent?'

And she turned to me, gave me a smile and the twinkle in her eyes returned – I cannot remember my mother laughing aloud that often, but I will always remember her grin. 'Flash your lights, honk your horn and reverse!' she said.

We all came back to England, and Mum passed away without her chemotherapy ever properly starting. Months afterwards, I found her afro comb, one side of the folding handle red, the other side green, grey hair still entangled around the steel prongs. Even the pharmacist whose shop she must have bought it from nearly cried when I told him the news. I put the comb away carefully in a black case, ready for the days when I would need to take it out and touch something that belonged to her.

My girlfriend cut my hair and held me in my grief. In her cottage, we danced together slowly, her body pirouetting around my near-motionless frame. I smelt the flowers in her perfume, and her blouse brushed my face, fanning the impulse to sneeze caused by the floating orphans from my scalp. Her movements wrapped around me like mine had cradled my sons as they sat high on a stool, a descendant of the chair my father had placed me on a long time ago.

No buzzing trimmer for my children, at least not at first – just the snip-snip of appropriated kitchen scissors trying to evenly reduce hair alien to my own, bouncy and frizzy in its big, circular waves. I graduated to an electric instrument like the high-street hairdressers and thought my work was not bad at all until one day, glancing away for the smallest moment, I carved a runway across the youngest's innocent head. That son's hair was now an explosion of locks and too much for me to handle even if he would let me, which he would not – glares and blackmail on my part failed against the resolve of his self-expression. A rebellion which I thought would please my father very much.

My father did not want to stay under cold, grey clouds, and after my mother's funeral, my brother, sister and I made arrangements to bring him back to the island. All the important possessions too large to go in his suitcases were barrelled up and shipped over, but he kept with him the clippers that he proudly told everyone in the village he had got my brother to buy on the internet for him.

A few months after my siblings had settled him in, my girlfriend and I flew over to see how things were going. I drilled, swept and cut, looking after my father's house and head, and once again the stubborn outgrowths in his nose.

Many journeys separated this trip from my exile here as a child. My parents had sent us to Saint Vincent as children to stay with relatives while they tried to lay the foundations of a new life in the States, she by travelling ahead to work as a nurse in Texas while my father stayed behind in Luton to sell the house and settle their affairs. It was a painful separation, and grief and hurt would always be some part of my bond with the island. Ghosts were never far away, and I did not have to be able to see the cemetery which overlooked the sea to feel them watching me. But this place and these people were inextricably in my blood and integral to the man I had become, not just the child I had been. I reverted easily to being 'back home', settling into island rhythms as if it were my time growing up in England that had been the interruption.

I wandered the village of many churches and remembered getting ready for Sunday school in an even smaller place with little benefit of electricity, dressed in my immaculate short-sleeved shirt and trousers, creases pressed rigidly straight, a geometrically precise parting in my hair like those of the other boys walking alongside the girls in their pure-white dresses.

All this came back to me, but I could not remember who had cut my hair back then. But now it was my girlfriend, her hair damp with sweat after ironing clothes outside in the sunshine. This was something new in village life, but nobody said a word or minded. She sorted and cleaned and rearranged a cupboard in a way that somehow brought my father to tears of gratitude, knowing that my mother would have been so pleased too. At night, my girlfriend slapped down dominoes with my father on the porch table and swallowed cold tins of Hairoun, showing full appreciation of the beer like the Vincentian she was becoming.

We went on a family trip out of the village, an expedition party squeezed into two cars, and my cousin braided my girlfriend's hair on the rainforest slopes of the emerald volcano. As she combed and plaited, my cousin shyly confessed that she had never before weaved a white woman's hair. Not many white Europeans ever ventured to this part of the island unless they had family here, which was shown by the schoolchildren waving excitedly to the 'English' lady they saw staying at my parents' house. My girlfriend, like my mother, always waved back.

My girlfriend cut my hair in the heat of the Caribbean sun while my father sat in his usual plastic chair, walking stick hanging on the handle of the open kitchen door and his lunchtime beer on the table. The little portable radio in front of him pinged out the tinny sounds of calypso. The music never really changing, yet somehow always different. A set of shiny new darts also lay there, brought over by me to satisfy my father's eagerness to pierce the weather-beaten board hanging in the corner, its staples and dividers corroded by 'sea moss' as they called it on this windward coast. He wanted to be 'Simply The Best' again, the soubriquet given to him over years of smoky Luton match nights and now stitched into the red baseball cap he wore about the house.

He had loved telling the friendly, younger regulars in the Irish pub how he used to rule the roost and oche there before they were even born. He bragged how once he and his brother Erdrin had gone to a pub in the town that was new to them. Their presence had been noted but tolerated until my father chalked his name up on the list of challengers for the dartboard, and taking on the regulars, he had proceeded to beat them all soundly one by one. However, the locals did not take kindly to these Black men pricking their pride and prestige and made it threateningly clear to the two brothers that their continued presence was not welcome. My dad and Erdrin had to make a hasty exit, still grinning though at my father's triumph.

In reality, my father's passion for the game could not be held up by his unreliable legs now, and it was only me who gave his arrows some exercise. Swarms of hungry sandflies hovered above Jerry, one of my parents' two dogs, dozing on the concrete floor of the porch in the shade. Tiger, the other, slept under a chair, quietly ecstatic that my father, even if alone, was here to spoil them with leftovers and treats in a most un-Vincentian style. The dogs in their ways were English now too.

The night before, I had argued with my father on the porch while rain swirled in the wind and our raised voices were only just cloaked by the TV perched on the concrete outside the bar next door for those who had none. Night creatures were drawn in by the lights, and the pale gecko which lived under the base of a lamp attached to the wall peered out intermittently and waited patiently as moths fluttered nearby.

Our dispute was about who my father would allow to support and cook for him now that my mother was not there to. But he never held a grudge, and the next day I cut his hair again, this time thousands of miles away from that Hightown living room where my mother had tried hard not to get involved in the ritual, concentrating on her word search. Now we both had to get used to life without having her there to rescue us. But somehow as I trimmed and shaved, I still heard my mother chivvying me to get a towel to catch the clippings or laughing and telling my father to stop with his foolishness when he bragged to the world that the hair on his head still grew so strong.

Flash your lights. Honk your horn. Reverse. My girlfriend and I departed the island leaving my father to continue his life there, connected to his children by phone calls and WhatsApp and the oversight and voices of a whole village. Now he would spend afternoons sitting in a worn recliner on his porch listening to the Atlantic swoosh beyond the palm trees and watching the villagers pass by below. Waiting for the shouts of appreciation and greeting that came up from the street below or the phone calls from England from my brother, sister and I, who were separated from him once more.

When my girlfriend and I left, my father waved down from the balcony as our car pulled away. It felt like the start of a new chapter, both for him and for us. We flew back to the UK and drove back to our homes, both of us knowing that continued separation was no longer an option. Now my girlfriend cuts my hair in a Kentish garden on the hottest summer's day. The breeze soothes my face as wisps of hair fly off like pollen into the haze of the sunshine, perhaps seeking another scalp on which to plant themselves. She cuts my hair, and I know I will never have a different barber again.

Parrots

Through the windowpane I saw a flash of yellow as wings unfurled and then settled back into camouflaged invisibility. The brief glimpse was like that of the leaves falling back to the ground between the bare branches of the South London trees whose buds were only just beginning to appear. Late-winter sunshine streamed over the leaves of the red poinsettia on the kitchen windowsill, a late starter which had not yet realised that winter was almost past.

As I looked over the lawn from my first-floor window, I wondered where all the daisies from the evening before had gone. But when I strode out in an old pair of slippers and picked up a single green feather from the grass, there they were: petals tightly bound and heads bowed as if waiting for the sun in prayer. I had never realised before that plants as commonplace as daisies could rise and fall so quickly. What secret or sustenance their tiny leaves were hiding, I did not know.

The only thing in England I had as comparison for this natural reflex was the automatic response of humble woodlice, which in my childhood I would prod and disturb so that I could see them curl up into balls and roll them a few inches with the flick of a fingertip. But in Saint Vincent there had been all kinds of natural phenomena to expand my schoolboy awareness: there I would play with moss, lichen or some such tiny plant along the roadside and watch it recoil and clench. In Saint Vincent there were giant land snails the size of my foot, bug-eyed praying mantises which I kept in jars and fed unlucky spiders to, vicious hornets, and the rodent manicou and agouti, which I heard spoken about as a rare treat to be caught, cooked and eaten but never saw myself. Saint Vincent was full of wonders for me. Back then I also found out that Saint Vincent held horrors.

In London at this time of year, before the leaves fully returned, I could see through the gaps in the branches to the houses on the far side of the trees and the people living inside them. A man my age mirrored my movements as I dried and put away the washing-up, his glass-fronted kitchen looking out on a much bigger garden than the square of grass behind my rented accommodation.

In the distance, a collapsed pyramid of blue, red and green material lay against the winter-stained window of a conservatory, perhaps a dismantled tent or a forgotten and propped-up kite. In the middle distance, against the trunk of a tree, there was another clump of green and yellow feathers, clinging to the gnarled bore like a migrant woodpecker. In the copse of trees beyond the back fence, the parakeets communicated in squawks and whistles, chattering and crying as they harassed each other or errant magpies. They only come down low to burgle my cheap Asda bird feeder, scaring away the corpulent and passive garden pigeons.

There were many urban legends to explain these troops of exotic birds which clustered across London and swooped and swirled across its suburban back gardens. One said that the parakeets had escaped from the set of *The African Queen*, which was partly shot in Ealing in 1951, presumably to create scenes simulating environments which were deemed too dangerous to expose Bogart and Hepburn to in Uganda where the rest of the movie was filmed. Imported parakeets were allowed to fly and squawk above the film sets of artificial reeds and water tanks, but seemingly some had made their escape.

There was another claim that the first birds were released by Jimi Hendrix on London's Carnaby Street in the 1960s. Alternatively, some said that the massive and unpredicted storm that struck the UK in 1987 also split birdhouses and aviaries asunder so that hundreds of birds were able to escape into the wild.

The mundane reality researchers had more recently settled on was that pet birds had separately and periodically been released both accidentally and deliberately, these escapees spanning back to Victorian times and having nothing to do with publicity stunts by musicians or movie stars. A friend of mine loved this story and liked to imagine the birds as a small community of escapees and liberated creatures, gathering and growing.

Seeing the birds swoop across my garden reminded me of a tall, plastic parrot which in the 1970s took pride of place in my family's immaculate front room in Luton. The Saint Vincent parrot (*Amazona guildingii*) was designated national bird on the same day that the island obtained political independence from the British – 27 October 1979. My parents placed their model on the glass-fronted dresser containing all the best and hardly-ever-used plates and glasses, standing on a gold perch, the better to show off its livery of red, blue and yellow feathers.

Another piece of 'home' in the room was the map on the wall. It lay flat against the orange-striped wallpaper which offset the peach settee and cushions. Black tapestry unfurled from a plastic tube, the words at the top proclaiming in large white capitals 'SOUVENIR OF' and continuing at the bottom 'SAINT VINCENT AND THE GRENADINES'. The main island was embedded in a black cloth sea, whilst below and to the right a gaggle of smaller islets floated in train to their brown-tinted parent, dolphins and flying fish bouncing in the waves around their shores. Both a galleon and yacht cruised the waters between the islands, traversing both space and time. Place names floated in italicised font above indentations in the coastline and at the bends and terminations of rivers. *Layou. Georgetown. Owia. Walliabou. Kingstown. Biabou.* Most of the village and towns were dotted close to where the white-tipped waves lapped the palm-flecked beaches. Inland, ripples and contours marked the rise of ancient peaks. And near the top of the island, the cone of a mountain rose to its summit crowned by a blue crater lake and simply marked *La Soufrière*.

It was not until I was an adult that I found out that the colours of our replica and the long and elegant tail feathers stretching almost down to the dresser top bore little resemblance to the birds formally depicted in guidebooks and on websites.

The wild parrots mirrored the national flag with their feathers' hues of yellow, green and blue as well as brown, but perhaps for my parents in their yearning for reminders of home, any parrot would do. This one held on to the horizontal bar not through a bond of plastic melted onto metal but because the long, black, ridged talons curled around it with an impressively implacable grip. They could be prised loose though with dogged childhood persistence so that the large bird could be cuddled like a baby. This punishable offence and the risk of its painful consequences needed the surety of both our parents being occupied at the very far end of the garden.

The vivid colours of the plastic feathers were a magnet for my brother, sister or me if we were able to sneak into the sacrosanct space of the front room while our parents were distracted with cooking, watching telly or gardening. A ferocious beak, curved and severe enough to crush nuts and tear into coconut husks, curved out from beneath the huge, amber eyes which radiated a hypnotic gaze from deep within its static frame. A favourite dare was to insert my finger, or even better a sibling's finger, between the scimitar curves of the black top and lower beak. I would then simply pause until an unsubtly disguised jerk gave an imitation of life to the plastic frame and caused my sister or brother to wriggle free and run screaming from the room.

In 1996, I went back to Saint Vincent for the first time in twenty years. Amongst all the fears and tensions about finding the demons of my childhood there, I looked forward to being able to explore the lush island, to finding waterfalls, climbing the volcano and letting my bare feet feel black sand between my toes again. I wondered if I might see the national bird in the wild too, the real-life version of the figure that had stood on my parents' front-room dresser. But although I went on journeys far and wide, off and on road, the closest I got was hearing calls high above as we walked a forest trail deep in the Vermont Valley. The birds that my guidebook informed me were making the noises stayed invisible in the treetops.

I would have settled for those sounds, but then, as I was returning from a beach trip, I saw a live Vincentian parrot for the first time, forlorn and bedraggled in a cage outside a bar. It was not poked or mistreated but lonely, dreaming of the echoes of the rainforest valleys where it could call to invisible kin hidden miles away in the dense canopies and swoop and plunder fruit without ever being disturbed by the people and the fumes of cars. A chain around its ankle was long enough for it to be able to reach the sides of its monkey-sized cage, and parents would swoop to rescue stumbling toddlers before podgy digits were inserted through the frame to tease it. But this parrot moved very slowly, and, like its artificial cousin in Luton, mostly not at all.

Other versions of the Saint Vincent parrot came into my life as I grew and my adult responsibilities increased. After my parents returned to live in Saint Vincent, I sometimes propped one of my father's old, plastic driving licences on my desk. The national bird stared out from the back, its head yellow, bands of green, red and brown circling beneath before its body ended in startling blue tail feathers. It was a souvenir of Saint Vincent and a daily reminder of him.

Close by there was another version: a clay parrot made at school by my youngest son, which sat or rather leant over to one side on my bookshelf. It was broad of face with a great band of yellow running down its otherwise green body, punctuated by blobs of black, repeating triangles placed snowman-like for its eyes and beak. The feet were misshapen but still functional statements of a determination to hold on.

In 2019, my girlfriend Julie and I lay on our blanket in the shade of what I hoped was not one of the manchineel trees whose innocent-seeming leaves we had been warned not to touch. Behind our spot was a derelict villa, seemingly uninhabited, except for the occasional shirtless youth who used it as a shortcut to get down to the beach, often smiling at us, always friendly.

During the morning, I made several trips to get beers, sometimes having to wade into the warm water to get past rocks and then ouching and ahhing as I padded across the hot sand to a little vendor's cabin. The locally brewed and delicious Hairouns were sold out, and I had to make do with bottles of Grenadian lager, the lady in the cabin lending me her bottle opener on the promise I would bring it back. It was when I was returning from one of these forays that I noticed the wheelchair. It sat empty and abandoned at the end of the road which dipped down from the highway to the beach, like the enflowered ghost bicycles left by fallen riders which stood chained to railings alongside busy roads back in London, sometimes adorned with a fading photograph.

I had also bought chicken curry and rice in polystyrene boxes from the stall next door – these we quickly 'nyamed' down with plastic forks and spoons. Our food eaten, Julie stretched out on the blanket and fell asleep in the sunshine. I simply sat up, shifting off the blanket so that I could bury my toes in the sand, and stared into the blue waters, the beachgoers who passed in front of me minor distractions, like the gulls that swooped and soared.

Beyond the secluded inlet of Indian bay, the Grenadines trailed away towards the horizon. Thirty-two islands and cays made up the country, and five were in sight. Closest and within sea taxi or hardy swimming distance were Fort Duvernette and the private splendour of Young Island, both dwarfed by the imposing bulk nine miles away of the second-largest island after Saint Vincent itself, Bequia.

Further away, low but still clear where the sea met the sky, were Battowia, and the small bump of Balliceaux. Barren Balliceaux was where in 1796, the year after the death of their Chief Chatoyer, 5,080 of the Garinagu who had continued to fight on were exiled by the Crown as punishment for their resistance. Without fresh water, vegetation or arable soil, and still tortured and mistreated by their captors, over 2,000 prisoners died there.

In 1797, the British sent ships to transport the remaining Garinagu into a further exile which would last centuries beginning on Roatan Island, off the coast of Honduras. Only 2,026 of the original 5,000 prisoners survived to be taken to shore on Roatan on 12 April 1797. As the Garinagu community grew, their resilience enabled them to spread to Belize and other parts of Central America, but they never forgot where they had come from. Now, like me, they were reaching out to their origins and tracing their path home.

A disturbance in the lapping waves broke my reverie and brought me back to our place on the beach in the hot sun. The man was floating, and seeing how he calmly let the sea rock him, my thoughts came back to the wheelchair that I had seen further down the beach. He was not far out, just beyond where I had already waded out to so I could stand while Julie took photos from the shore. *Just chilling like us*, I thought, in the azure dapples of Indian Bay. The lowering sun was burning my skin now, so I too went back into the water.

Near us, closer to the shore, there was another Black family in the waves, a little boy bobbing in a green rubber ring and a woman and three men floating in the sea around him, worshipping him. Like the little boy, I splashed and played, plunging myself backwards and floating, my hands cupping handfuls of water under the surface, the most confident swimming stroke I could ever execute. There was another family, a little girl bobbing in the water with her mum and dad, and she loudly and without concern asked them why Julie was a different colour from all the rest of us bathers.

The floating man bobbed closer, and we chatted a while as the waves washed and cooled us.

'Ah where yuh from?' he asked me. 'Englan'? Englan'? If all the Vincy people in Englan' come back ah wey we ah go put dem?' But he was smiling and welcoming me back rather than questioning why I was there.

His brother swam out to us and held him up, and now I noticed that his head was buoyed by an orange inflatable. His brother bathed his paralysed legs with the seawater, and they told me that he had become paraplegic after being chopped with a cutlass in a fight. In Saint Vincent, the rum-fuelled confrontations seemed less frequent but often even more brutal than the sprees of knife crime back in London.

'Yuh cud len' ah likkle change to help ah brudda?' the floating man asked, but truly I had no change to give.

Later I saw his brother further down the beach harpooning strange-finned fish and retrieving conch shells from the sandy bottom of the bay. When Julie woke and we packed up to return to our car, I asked her what money she had, and she found ten dollars deep in her purse. But when we waded our way along the beach in between the rocks, the wheelchair had gone. Its absence was a sign that I had no part to play here, no responsibility, no duty. This was a new thing for me. For a long time, my default reaction had been that if I saw what I thought was need, I had to be the one to respond – to help, to guide… to fix.

After I qualified as a social worker, my career focus had initially been in working with Deaf and disabled people. Because I could not stand being alone with my own disruption and anger, I sought peace in helping others – in social work, community development and the voluntary sector. Calm came, but the pain never went away. I kept seeing mirrors of myself – boys who I thought had been harmed and stereotyped like I had been. And thinking that I had to rescue them, I projected my unresolved experiences of hurt and loss into the life frames of others. Tragedy unnerved and uncoupled me and left me plunging when I thought about the loss of a positive future for other young people. I wanted to take responsibility for everyone who had been hurt, who were bullied or neglected.

I met young people and adults who were experiencing mental health problems or the threatening clouds of these but who had no one to listen patiently to them or lean on as their ability to manage unravelled, their vulnerability leading to further risks. Teenagers who since childhood had been given unceasing messages that failure was not an option and so unsurprisingly could not tolerate any possibility of it; if they felt exposed or judged, jokes and amiability might melt and erupt into aggressive fury. Many of those young people were Black young men who shouted out loudly the colours they saw in the world, but the world heard only snarls. And reacted accordingly.

What I also encountered was hope and possibility being realised as young people, families, professionals and volunteers worked together to find a way for them back to stability and inclusion. I was lucky because I was given a chance to see the potential of so many realised through their own verve and self-perseverance, and especially to have my awareness enriched and broadened by the wisdom, perspectives and self-determination of disabled people.

It was not only people who bonded through geography and place of birth who could come together to fight for their identity, rights, culture and independence. I saw young disabled people become writers and readers, artists and activists, speakers and creators. Saw them represent their communities and peers and tell those providing services how to do it better and get it right. I got to watch them have fun too and do the things that so many non-disabled children and young people took for granted: go on residentials, get an award in assembly, mess around in a disco with their mates, fall in love with each other and simply have a laugh.

Julie and I walked back towards our car, splashing through the shallow water which had encroached between the rocks marking the end of the beach. I hoped that the spirits of George and his mother were close too – that somehow they had waded through the seawater back to the island where they both were born. I had a feeling that the ghosts of many other lost souls were here too, waiting in the shallows. All of them blown here by the Atlantic wind, the same one which urges the sea into breaking its back on the shoreline and rocks and then puts the waves back together, to begin their journey again. I still wanted all the young people who felt broken or ignored to find a way to feel whole again. I just knew now though that they would have to choose their own path and tide.

A group of Seventh Day Adventists had gathered by a small jetty, all adorned in their Saturday best, the ladies using parasols to shield themselves from the heat of the afternoon sun. We watched as the pastor and a younger man helped an elderly man in a blue robe with a light-blue collar walk into the waters of Indian Bay. When all were immersed to the bottoms of their chests, the pastor placed an arm around the shoulder of the man being baptised and another against his midriff.

'Ezekiel Jeremiah, I baptise you in the name of the father, the son and the Holy Spirit,' the pastor said loudly enough to carry his words over the swish of the sea and pushed the elderly man firmly backwards and beneath the water. For a moment, only the white of the pastor's robes was visible before Ezekiel was brought to the surface again. As he waded back to the beach and his new church family, I wondered about his journey and about what had brought him here today at this time in his life to seek renewal.

Julie said she would drive, and I sat quietly in the little jeep on the way back to Biabou washed by waves of self-reflection. I thought about the men in the sea and how we were all broken, me included. My pain was expressed first through heartrending grief but then the blows of my fist and feet, and I wondered whether if I had stayed on the island past childhood, the heft of a cutlass would have found its way into my hand too.

'Shall we stop for something to eat, hon?' said Julie, breaking into my reverie, and we scanned either side of the road for enticing possibilities before turning off the coastal highway down to a cluster of familiar-looking buildings. We parked and sat to eat outside on the terrace of a hotel, a warm breeze ruffling the heat. The sea view was beautiful, and I felt better already. The same way I had felt being back on the island.

I still felt sad on so many mornings, but something else had seeped into me in the Caribbean: the flavours and memory of the food, the relatives who had only smiles and welcoming connection for me, the lilt which crept back into my body and voice, and the willingness to spend time doing nothing which enfolded my body. I had climbed up the hill and brought my grief with me, but this time its weight was like being leant on by an old friend. Some things can be broken but still remain whole.

I knew my anxieties were about the future. About what would become of all of those I cared about if benevolent entities were not there to look out for and watch over us. Now I could believe that there would probably always be that someone. Those friends, lovers or family who would take care of us without taking over or taking charge. I realised that I might be alright and, if I allowed it, the world would find a way to accept the people I worried about and me as we were. That I did not have to rescue anyone.

I had a mental image of one of the young people I had met standing proud and happy with the artwork he had come in to collect and cracking a joke about the staff making up excuses to bring him in so that they could see him. I still worried about his future in a world which was careless with the potential of young and disabled people. But at last, I was hopeful.

I passed through the air-conditioned cool of the hotel reception and when I stepped outside to the car park I realised suddenly that I had been here before. I had missed it on our way in but now looked right, down a cloistered passageway, and saw the cage still standing there, twenty-five years on from my last visit. It could not possibly be the same occupant, I thought, and indeed a younger, cockier bird now strutted inside, its feathers shinier and containing more grey. It jumped from side to side of its enclosure, squawking and lively, and, whether for food or curiosity, used its taloned feet to clamber close to where I was, an iridescent eye always keeping me in sideways view.

For some reason I put my hand on the outside of the cool metal and felt my finger stretching towards a specific square of the fencing, uncurling and extending. I wanted the bite to wake me up and perhaps to punish me for all my transgressions, for the anger and the fights and for cutting off those who loved me the most. I wanted to endure trial through the threat of its bite and see who would react first, me or the parrot.

And then I felt Julie's hand on my shoulder, pulling me back. 'Come on, baby – it's time to go home.'

Farewells

Mum sat on the bench in the autumn sunlight as I knelt trying to pull out the tussocks of deep-rooted weeds which seemed to need just the faintest mist of a drizzle to burst into life and take over the grass. I wrestled with the leaves and tubers which were buried deep in the earth, trying to stop my jeans sliding off the plastic bag I had placed under my knees to stop my trousers getting dirty. Somehow, I had forgotten the cushion which I normally had in that self-same bag along with the trowel and hand fork I packed for exactly this kind of work.

It was autumn, my favourite season, and around us the browns, reds and golden hues of the leaves on the trees were a kaleidoscope of death and renewal.

'How you get on with that little boy?' Mum asked.

'George, you mean? The boy buried in Marlow?'

'Yes, the one you went to see.'

'I found him, Mum. It was hard, but I found his grave.'

'That's good. Did you learn much?'

I paused for a moment and watched the other people I could see close to and around us, all lost in their thoughts and tending.

'I wondered what it meant to his mother, Mum.. To lose him like that. What she would do to get him back?'

Now my mother was quiet too, her eyes following a mini-arc to track the passage of everyone who passed by on the path in front of us and, if they were also elderly and female, sometimes sharing a nod and a half-smile.

'I found out about some other Vincentians too, Mum,' I told her.

'Really? Who?'

'There was a lady called Annie Brewster. She was a nurse at the Royal London in Whitechapel, well it was the London Hospital, back then, in the 1880s and '90s.'

'It must have been hard to be Black and a nurse back then. I never knew Vincentians came here from so far back.'

'I think it might have been tough, although they seem to have loved her. They called her the Nurse Ophthalmic. That's the ward she worked on, Mum.'

'Ahhh, that is hard work. How long she work there for?'

'Twenty years, Mum. She died when she was forty-three.'

'That's sad. Was she a matron? A sister?'

'I don't think so.'

'Ah, it was the same for me. I never wanted to be the one telling people what to do. I just wanted to get on with my job with the mothers and babies. How they treat her?'

'I think they liked her, but you know what? I saw the records and it said that when she first joined, she failed her nurse's examination because she had had a "lamentably poor education", or so they said! This was the daughter of a businessman, Mum. She had travelled the world already. And I saw a letter written

in her name to the *London Daily News*. It was the best writing
ever! Like a posh lady writing. I don't think she ever had a poor
education. I just think they assumed she did.'

My mum sucked her teeth. 'That's how these things work.'

'There was one more Vincentian boy. Back in the early 1900s.'

My mum laughed. 'Where all these Vincys come from?'

I smiled too. 'This boy was called George Egbert Robinson.
Bertie, they called him. This lord and lady brought him over
from Saint Vincent to be a footman at their stately home in
Yorkshire – Harewood House – in 1893 when he was thirteen.
The lord and lady's family said that when these people were
over visiting their estates, this old woman ran after them and
left this young boy with them. I travelled up there to find out
more about him. It's an amazing place, Mum. Like a palace.
They know though that so much of their wealth must have
come from the slaves and lands they owned in the Caribbean.'

'And how he get on with them?'

'Well, okay for a long while, I think. He was with them for
nearly thirty years. Although it's weird: the Lascelles – that was
the rich family – took him back to Saint Vincent in 1906 and
left him to be with his family again. But he didn't want to stay
it seems and made it back to England on his own.'

'That's strange. What was going on there?'

'I don't know, Mum. He or maybe the Lascelles used to send
money back to help his family all the time. Maybe they needed
his wage, or maybe he just couldn't settle after being in England
so long.'

My mum shook her head. 'His mother would have been so pleased to see him though. Her heart would have broken twice to lose him all over again.'

We were both quiet for a while.

'What happened to him after he get back to England?'

'Well, then in 1922, he got a maid from another well-off household pregnant, and he stole fifty pounds for her and his baby. They caught him and made him leave the country or they would have handed him over to the police.'

'Where did he go?' my mum asked.

'Trinidad, Mum. He caught a boat there from Dover. No one knows why. Maybe it was just the first ship he could catch going somewhere he might know. Maybe someone promised him some work out there. But no one ever heard from him again.'

My mum nodded. 'Yes. Trinidad not so far from Saint Vincent. Lots of Vincentians travel there.'

'But did you know the last two weeks before he left England he was in Southampton. I didn't understand why he went there either. But seems there have been Vincentians there for a long, long time. From since 1796, when they brought some Garinagu prisoners back to Hampshire who had fought the British. Prisoners of war, not slaves. They put them in Portchester Castle.'

My mum nodded. 'Yes, me hear that too. Where they put them foot down, Vincentians always find a way to make it through. Despite all the struggles.'

She waited a while and then she asked me another question. 'So he left his baby?'

'Yes, Mum. Sad, isn't it? I don't think he ever made it back, no. I wonder if he wanted to though? If that was his plan all along?'

My mum looked at me. 'Parents always want to return, it's just that some never make it. Things get in the way. They make mistakes or are stubborn, can't do right for doing wrong. Like they say – "dem who can't hear, feel". But they never forget those they had to leave behind. Especially when it's their children who they can't take with them. They never stop wanting to be together again, some way. And they always keep on, keep on trying. That's why we Vincentians always say we're coming back, God willing.'

I thought about what Mum had said. About Bertie, Annie, George and Catherine – how despite what they had lost, they were still here as the ancestors, the witnesses, the ghosts of the past. They encircled and looked after all of us who were trying to make our way home perhaps because they never could themselves.

'Yes, we do, don't we, Mum?' I said with a smile and started to gather up the tools I had been using to pull out the weeds and thorns. Then, in my dream, I kissed her on the forehead like I did on the night she passed away and squeezed her hand. 'Goodbye, Mum. I coming back.'

EPILOGUE

Lin

1963, Highgate

The city falls away beneath her, masked by more hues of green than she could ever have imagined when she was at school in Georgetown, reading about the Mother Country at her wooden desk. This green and pleasant land indeed. She loves coming here when she can on her lunch break, to this park which hovers above London. As she eats, she sometimes reads a romantic novel or revises and makes notes for her studies. But more often her eyes explore the history laid out before her. She watches the walkers and the people still brave enough to sit out on the grass, while beyond the treeline the city spreads out like an ocean. She tries to put a name to points she can recognise – Saint Paul's, Big Ben, the rising modernity of the GPO tower – and imagines the outings she and the boy from Biabou will have to the ones she does not know.

She draws her coat tighter around her. It is sunny but still cold outside, and the invisibility of her breath does not last past her nose. When she closes her eyes, the chill wind is still there on her face, and she can feel all her possibilities swirling around her and stirring inside. Sometimes at night as she slept, she dreamt of walking along black sand beaches and seeing whales basking in the warm Atlantic currents around islands bathed in mist. But when she awoke, all her plans were on the life she could build here in this cold land. She could not imagine when she might see Saint Vincent again.

The boy from Biabou was coming to see her tonight. He would walk to come lime and relax with her in her small room two or three times a week, come rain or shine, all the way from Dalston to Archway. His hands often still smelt of the grease and oil from the trains or the coal he piled into the engines, but she didn't mind that now. And if, as sometimes happened, she was late finishing her shift, she knew her handsome Vincentian would be there waiting for her. He would wait in the kitchen with the other girls on her floor and make them laugh and smile too, but it was only when his Lin walked in the door that his eyes would truly light up.

Somewhere in the distance, a bell sounds the hour and echoes across the park. She gets up from the bench, closes her notebook and tucks it into her coat pocket as she heads back down the hill to the hospital, ready for whatever her next shift will bring.

Historical Figures

George Alexander Gratton – 'The Beautiful Spotted Boy', July 1808–February 1813

'Catherine' – George's mother imagined, dates of birth and death unknown

John Richardson – English showman, 1767–November 1837

George 'Bertie' Robinson – 'The Footman from Saint Vincent', 8 November 1879–unknown

Annie Catherine Brewster – 'The Nurse Ophthalmic', 1858–February 1902

A Letter from Alexis

Dear reader,

Thank you so much for reading *Windward Family*. If you want to discover more inspirational memoirs from Thread you can sign up at the link below. Your email address will never be shared, and you can unsubscribe at any time.

www.thread-books.com/sign-up

I was inspired to start this book by the life story of one small boy from Saint Vincent, George Alexander Gratton, and its scope grew as I came across the lives, achievements and challenges faced by other members of the Vincentian diaspora as they made huge journeys around the world. As I set off on my personal exploration, I wanted the stories of those travellers to include the journeys of members of my own family. The foundation for the creation of *Windward Family* is my connection with people I am linked to through ties of love, kinship and history.

Windward Family is my attempt to give voice to the ghosts of my ancestors. Writing this book has been about linking with those who came before me and their stories and also about my bonds with those around me who shared my life experience in the places which are so important in *Windward Family*. Biabou and Saint Vincent, Luton, Whangārei and New Plymouth are central to this book and are why I call it a hymn to the small places – although I only mean 'small' in terms of how well they are known around the world.

Writing the stories which are part of *Windward Family* has meant success to me in ways which aren't about securing a publishing contract or getting an agent. Success was being invited back to my hometown of Luton to share my words with a group in the library which I used to wander as a teenager, never imagining that I would come back as a writer. Success was being asked to be the online guest of a group of writers on the island of Saint Vincent where my parents were born. Success is persuading people to listen to and read stories which have not been heard before.

The words in this book are my truth but may not be the whole truth, and I apologise for anything that I have misinterpreted or misrepresented in my eagerness to share these histories. The thoughts, words and reflections of the Vincentians George Egbert Robinson, George Alexander Gratton, George's mother Catherine and the English showman John Richardson are entirely imagined. I just thought that it was important in any way I could to try to bring them back to life.

I would love to hear from anyone who has an interest in any of the themes explored in *Windward Family* – it would be great to stay in touch. The best places to contact me via social media are:

@alexismontekeir

www.facebook.com/alexismontekeir

Other work: https://linktr.ee/alexiskeir

www.goodreads.com/author/show/20294816.Alexis_Keir

Acknowledgements

Windward Family is a canoe of memories which floated on and was carried forward by many benevolent and loving tides and currents. From the end to the beginning, these are just a few I want to express my gratitude for.

For their wise guidance and belief in me and the book, everyone at Thread, especially my patient editor, Nina Winters, and also Claire Bord, Maureen Cox, Alex Holmes and Peta Nightingale. Many thanks too to my friend David Kelly for all his hours of generously given advice as I set off on the path to publication, and to the Society of Authors for their accessible and expert knowledge and input.

I was blessed to receive detailed feedback, comments and unceasing support from my Vincentian family members and friends: Anita Brown, Kayon Keir, Erdrin Keir, Selwyn Keir, Michael Lewis, Keisha Phillips, Fitzroy and Judy Rogers, Monique Rogers, my cousin Angela Leach and my mother's sisters Lucette, Margaret, Mavis and Stella. I am also very grateful for the encouragement of Lois Wright, daughter of Mrs Dorrel Wright, the dear friend of our family.

I was continually supported by the Writers for Saint Vincent Group who are so diverse in their creativity, talents and skills. I would like to note especially Cecil Browne, Peggy Carr, Lafleur

Cockburn, Andoni Castillo Perez, H. Nigel Thomas and Michael McMillan for their advice on the contents of the book. All are wonderful creators whose huge personal achievements did not stop them from leaning down to offer a hand and guidance to me.

My dear close friends in Aotearoa warmly welcomed me to their land and enabled me to feel like I had found new homes in Northland and Taranaki. Their embrace contributed so much to me having a happy time in those beautiful places. I am so grateful to those people who gave me specific advice and feedback on aspects of living in Aotearoa and of Māori culture, including Natalee Burkhardt, Rose Cameron, Allan Cobham, Lynda Coley, Margie Davis, Paula Frost, Karen Johns, Maryann Lee, Karen Tuck and David Younger.

My research was hugely dependent on the constantly kind support of those who pointed me in the direction of details and backgrounds that I could never have imagined uncovering on my own or being given access to. Those skilled researchers included Audrey Dewjee and Allison Edwards of the Leeds Diasporian Stories Research Group, Don John, Paula Martin of Harewood House, Kerwin Rodgers, Loraine Thomas, the staff of Barts Health NHS Trust Archives and Museums, and staff of the Parish Church of Saint Mary, Newington.

For their quiet and wise advice and mentoring, I am ever grateful to Rupert Lancaster of Hodder and Stoughton, and Anna Derrig, both of whom have become lifelong friends.

The platform on which I began *Windward Family* was the amazing and brilliant London Writers Awards programme run by Spread the Word. The help given by the staff I met through the programme was invaluable, including the continuous encouragement of Ruth Harrison, Bobby Nayyar, Eva Lewin, Kit Caless and my lovely friend Laura Kenwright. I also valued so much the feedback and encouragement from the writers in my non-fiction group as we worked together to push forward our writing dreams – writers from backgrounds underrepresented in publishing who are all so talented and whose words I look forward to reaching a wide audience too.

Windward Family has been finished whilst I took part in the London Library's Emerging Writers Programme 2021–2022, and I am very thankful for the help and support of Claire Berliner, Head of Programmes, and all the brilliantly kind staff at the London Library who were always so quick to respond to my queries and who enabled access to such an inspiring and reflective space to write and create in.

I would also like to thank my fellow Emerging Writers in the non-fiction group who gave me feedback on the final chapters of *Windward Family*, especially Grace Quantock for her always thoughtful and warm advice, and for sharing the highs and lows of being an emerging writer with me.

My thanks go to everyone connected with the wonderful online journal, *The Selkie*, who first published 'I Lands' in 2019, the story which became the foundation chapter of *Windward Family*. And I extend that same gratitude to *The Caribbean Writer*, who in 2021, selected 'My Girlfriend Cuts My Hair' for publication in their Volume 35.

I am hugely grateful to all the friends who have stayed with me on this road and supported me. Their names are too many to list in full, but I would like to especially give thanks for the unceasing support and kindness of Rosanna Cooper, Catherine Evans, Naomi Graham, Ceri Hunter, Yaseen Parkar and Sajjad Rashid who read early versions of the pieces which came together to form *Windward Family* and gave invaluable advice and encouragement to spur me on. Many thanks also to the Friday Night Pub for our deep friendship, which has always held me up through difficult times. From the Luton creative community, Lizzie Fretwell and Rae Leaver gave me great and much appreciated help to shape and share my stories. Also from Luton came the support of the strong, inspirational hockey players of Vauxhall who, as the saying goes, are 'much more than just a club'.

My truly inspirational high-school English teacher Mrs Doreen Thakoordin started things off for me a long time ago by always encouraging me to daydream, to imagine and to create stories. After my teenage years, somehow writing and I lost each other, but my passion was reignited in 2015 by entering a community writing programme, E17 Stories, run by Waltham Forest Council and facilitated by Amy Mason who, like Mrs Thakoordin, encouraged me to start putting my words down on the page. From that time until 2022 and the completion of *Windward Family*, I worked at the North London charity Elfrida Rathbone Camden, and I am so grateful to the staff and trustees there for always supporting my desire to write alongside doing my day job. My special appreciation goes to the close and supportive friends I made at ERC, Sade Alade and Chris McAuley.

All through the writing of this book, I have been buoyed by the never-ending love, support, feedback and patience of my wonderful partner Julie Brooks, who, as well as being amazing, is also the best barber this Luton boy has ever known. And this book is written as a gift to my beautiful sons Joshua and Tom as a reminder of all that they belong to and that belongs to them. Joshua, Julie, and Tom are my inspirations too.

This book is grounded in the love, appreciation and gratitude I hold for my mother, Lenore Henrietta Keir (née McBarnett), and my father, Jason Winston Keir, whose lives are at the heart of every single word. They encouraged me in all I have ever tried to do and always told me that they were proud of me.

Windward Family could not have been written in the way it has been without the unceasing support of my sister and brother, Alison David and Anthony Keir.

And it all began and comes back to all the people of Biabou, with especial love for Ann, Anthony, Donkeymeat, Judy, Fitzroy, Handyman, Hulk and Dobbin, with whom I had the most beautiful day out, and everyone else who held and remembered Monty when he came home.

This book is written with all homage and respect to my family's beautiful island known as Hairouna, Yurumein and Saint Vincent, my sea the wild Atlantic and my mountain La Soufrière. I give my thanks to all Saint Vincent's people now and forever and to those who laid the path for me to write this book.

My last thanks are to and in remembrance of all the 'barrel children' and are to salute their courage and perseverance and all the good they brought into the world after enduring such loss.

Until,
Alexis Monty Keir

Bibliography

Altick, Richard (1978) *The Shows of London.* Harvard University Press.

Fitzpatrick, Robert V.W. (2001) *Biabou: The Story of a Community.*

Hochschild, Adam (2012) *Bury the Chains: The British Struggle to Abolish Slavery.* Pan Books.

John, Don (2021) *Black Stories Southampton: Extraordinary Accounts.* Positive Message Limited.

John, Don and Muirhead, Stella (2010) *A Black History of Southampton: 16th Century to 21st Century.* Positive Message Limited.

Kirby, I.E. and Martin, C.I. (1972) *The Rise and Fall of the Black Caribs.* St. Vincent and the Grenadines National Trust.

McMillan, Michael (1997) *The Black Boy Pub and Other Stories.* Wycombe County Council.

McMillan, Michael (2009) *The Front Room: Migrant Aesthetics in the Home.* Black Dog Publishing.

Olusoga, David (2017) *Black and British: A Forgotten History.* Pan Books.

Rediker, Marcus (2007) *The Slave Ship: A Human History.* John Murray

Roberts, Jacqueline (2020) *The Beautiful Spotted Boy: George Alexander Gratton 1808–1813.* Jacqueline Roberts.

Scott, Dick (2008) *Ask That Mountain: The Story of Parihaka*. Raupo Publishing.

Spinelli, Joseph (1973) 'Land use and population in St. Vincent, 1763–1960. A contribution to the study of the patterns of economic and demographic change in a small West Indian island'.

Telfer, Bridget; Shepley, Emma and Reeves, Carole (eds) (2011) *Reframing Disability: Portraits from the Royal College of Physicians*. Royal College of Physicians.

Throssell, Harold (ed.) (1975) *Social Work: Radical Essays*. University of Queensland Press.

Toulmin, Vanessa (2019) 'Black circus performers in Victorian Britain'. *Early Popular Visual Culture*, volume 16, issue 3.

Waldegrave, Charles; Tamasese, Kiwi; Tuhaka, Flora and Campbell, Warihi (2003) *Just Therapy: A Journey*. Dulwich Centre Publications.

Walker, Alice (1997) *Anything We Love Can Be Saved*. W & N.

Williams, Eric (1984) *From Columbus to Castro: The History of the Caribbean, 1492–1969*. Vintage Books.